THE
CHALLENGE OF LEISURE

NRPA Recreation and Park Perspective Collection

edited by Dr. Diana R. Dunn
Director of Research
National Recreation and Park Association

Education through Play	Curtis, H.	$19.00
Education through Recreation	Jacks, L.	$13.00
Education by Plays and Games	Johnson, G.	$15.00
The New Leisure Challenges for the Schools	Lies, E.	$17.00
Play in Education	Lee, J.	$25.00
Play and Mental Health	Davis, J.	$15.00
Education through Recreation	Johnson, G.	$10.00
The Practical Conduct of Play	Curtis, H.	$19.00
The Play Movement	Rainwater, C.	$21.00
The Play Movement and its Significance	Curtis, H.	$19.00
Playground Technique and Playcraft	Leland, A. & L.	$17.00
American Playgrounds	Mero, E.	$17.00
Leisure in the Modern World	Burns, C.	$15.00
The Threat of Leisure	Cutten, G.	$12.00
The Normal Course of Play	NRA	$16.00
The Education of the Whole Man	Jacks, L.	$12.00
The Challenge of Leisure	Pack, A.	$14.00
Off the Job Living	Romney, G.	$15.00
A Philosophy of Play	Gulick, L.	$16.00
Europe at Play	Weir, L.	$45.00
Music in American Life	Zanzig, A.	$28.00
Music in Institutions	Van de Wall, W.	$35.00
The First County Park System	Kelsey, F.	$15.00
County Parks	NRA	$14.00
Central Park—First Annual Report	New York	$14.00
The Spirit of Youth and the City Streets	Addams, J.	$12.00
Annals March 1910	AAP&SS	$16.00
Municipalization of Play and Recreation	Fulk, J.	$10.00
Luther Halsey Gulick	Dorgan, E.	$14.00
Constructive and Preventive Philanthropy	Lee, J.	$15.00

order from:

McGrath Publishing Company
Washington, D.C.

The
Challenge of Leisure

By

ARTHUR NEWTON PACK

•

McGrath Publishing Company

&

NATIONAL RECREATION AND PARK ASSOCIATION
WASHINGTON, D.C.

Library of Congress Cataloging in Publication Data

Pack, Arthur Newton.
    The challenge of leisure.

    1. Leisure. 2. United States—Social conditions.
3. Hobbies. I. Title.
BJ1498.P3 1972   175   72-1949
ISBN 0-8434-0438-8

ACKNOWLEDGMENT

Especial appreciation is due to Tom Gill for his aid in reading and amplifying much of the material contained in this book.

The author also gratefully acknowledges the assistance of Charles J. Phillips, an authority upon hobbies, particularly philately.

To certain publications the author has had frequent recourse. These are mentioned in the text.

CONTENTS

PART ONE
Leisure Confronts the Nation

PART TWO
Some Social Implications

PART THREE
A Few Words in Conclusion

PART ONE

LEISURE CONFRONTS THE NATION

I

THE DISCOVERY OF LEISURE

Not for always has living been recognized as an art.

That came only when man had attained the time and capacity for reflection—when the tempo of life allowed him to think not only "what shall I do?" but also "how, and why?" And this change in life's tempo has taken on a new significance in recent years. It is one of the strange things that have happened in our time—it is at one with mechanical developments, with spiritual and mental revaluations, and is resulting in new views of life itself.

None, certainly, has been stranger or more replete with potentialities for change than the rediscovery of leisure. Slowly creeping upon us in a manner little suspected because so easily absorbed in small quantities, leisure now rises to confront us as a new problem, and what was once regarded as the chief reason and goal of man's age-old

3

struggle for wealth may soon become the lot of every one of us—whether we like it or not.

And precisely because this newly discovered leisure promises to become the universal fate of man, it has been widely and diversely discussed in editorials and magazines. It has become news. It has even become a political issue, one of the various features of the New Deal that can comfortably be discussed without the bitterness inherent in other current problems. The New Leisure has become a subject for the appointment of committees, the compiling of statistics, the conducting of nation-wide surveys. As a slogan for advertising, it has even been widely publicized—and with good reason. That simple phrase "New Leisure," comes to depression-worn mankind with almost irresistible seduction, and it is easily adapted to almost any preconceived purpose, especially because no one seems to understand exactly what it means.

Just what is this New Leisure then? Manufacturers of cigarettes will tell you it is time that can be well spent smoking ever greater quantities of cigarettes—provided, of course, you smoke the particular brand they represent. Steamship and railroad companies will tell you it is an opportunity for more travel. It is time to attend more movies, to beautify your school-girl complexion,

4

time to read books and magazines, time to invest
in guns, fishing tackle, skis. Time, in short, to buy.
The list is endless. For as usual the industrious
gentlemen with an eye ever focused on the main
chance were not tardy in diverting this succulent
phrase, "New Leisure," into possibilities of increased dividends in their own line of endeavor.

But this—the multitudes of energetic advertisers to the contrary—may not be the chief *raison
d'être* of leisure, and we ourselves may have
greater ambitions than merely to become the outlets for producers' wares. And especially we
should like to know if leisure is to be anything
more than a casual opportunity exploited by the
first manufacturer clever enough to seize it. We
should like to know if there is any real directing
purpose in this new leisure problem. Has it a
fundamental economic end? What does it or what
could it mean in the pattern of our daily living?
What rôle could it conceivably play in terms of
increasing human happiness?

It may be that a glance into the past can give
us a clue to the future, but at the outset we might
as well admit that to us Americans the New
Leisure is actually something really new. There
may have been, as Ralph Borsodi states, in "This
Ugly Civilization," much more leisure during the

5

Middle Ages, when one third of the year consisted of holidays and festivals. There may have been more leisure on this continent in the pre-Columbian days when fat herds and opulent nature enabled the Maya and Toltec peoples and the great tribes to the north to build up systems of living that could only have been the fruit of enormous leisure. But so far as the history of the United States is concerned, there has never before been leisure—certainly not enough of it to constitute a problem.

We have been a leisureless nation. That may be why, in many respects, we have been a dour and rigid nation. And for all this there was reason enough. Our ancestors were too busy struggling against the wilderness, against the hostilities of a yet unmodified environment to have a moment to spare. The founders of this nation were confronted with tasks that in the early days of settlement at least presented problems that meant life or death to themselves and their dependents. It was work or starve. It was kill or be killed. Life for them was battle—and the battlefield is a poor breeding ground for leisure.

When the American pioneer read, studied or played, it was by the light of a home-made candle during hours really stolen from sleep, and at a

6

time when the physical exigencies of a long day
made reading or playing almost too expensive a
luxury. And here, too, the result was that what
little time he did spend was more often than not
directed to utilitarian ends—to prepare him better
for the battle of life—it wasn't really leisure.

Gradually, of course, the time came when he
had partially conquered his environment. Improved working tools enabled him to obtain his
living somewhat more easily, and left him with
a little surplus of physical energy and time. But
this did not create more leisure for the adult
members of his family. It only permitted the setting aside, first of hours, then of months, when
children might attend school and learn the simplest fundamentals of practical knowledge to prepare themselves in turn for the bitter struggle that
experience had taught them lay ahead. So far as
the adults were concerned, the little relaxation
they obtained came as a by-product of work, and
took such forms as quilting parties, barn raisings
—activities with a fundamentally utilitarian
basis. Of real leisure there was still none.

A sound fundamental basis exists for the fact
that the maxims and taboos of any race are generally based upon social necessity—they have, to
use a phrase of modern sociology, "survival value."

7

And it was also natural that the teachers and preachers of the pioneer order in America—mostly of the Puritan school—taught from the first that idleness was a sin, that all occupations, all spending, almost all thought which led to other than business success, as gauged by profits or by improved standards of living, was a social sin that should be exorcised, and which as a matter of fact during those early days was pretty carefully concealed or hidden. There was one consistent exception to this maxim—religion and church-going. But since these were considered as equally necessary preparations for the future, they too were of an essentially utilitarian character. They too had, in the very strictest sense, "survival value."

And perhaps that is why even today we are all of us a little ashamed of being caught in the act of doing nothing, so that we have only the courage to do nothing in groups—only the very old have gained either the wisdom or the justification that comes with the years to sit idly down and contemplate life as a spectacle, no longer obsessed with the seeming necessity for doing something about it.

So there arose in this country an aristocracy of toil. The rank and file of mankind was naturally intolerant of ease or any luxury, and they esteemed it to be a virtue to labor for its own sake. Conversely, leisure—the respite from labor—was vicious and not to be endured. Only as far back as 1839 one worthy pastor had this to say: "A man of leisure is one who has nothing to do—a condition supposed to be honorable in those countries where false forms of society make the many the servants of the few; but happily not in our own, where the greatest good to the whole number is the glorious aim of an intelligent democracy. Here the laborer is honorable, the idler infamous. We tolerate no drones in our hive. Sweat drops on the brow of honest toil are more precious than the jewels of a ducal coronet. We have no leisure, for the truly virtuous and faithful will find occupation for every moment."

This view of leisure as sinful and anti-social was strongly held at the opening of the nineteenth century when the first few machines were introduced, although for a long time no one recognized the inevitable results of these new inventions as causing an actual decrease in the requirement for human labor.

But those embryo machines that of themselves looked so unimportant and which had at most a slight but benign influence, were at no distant date to destroy the American tradition of work and to make necessary new and quite revolutionary conceptions of that "sinful" leisure. A growing irregularity of employment was already to be seen in the factory districts, but this was considered due to faulty management, to the greed of the factory owners, or to other human factors. There were as yet no Jeremiahs to announce to a busy continent that a fundamental and perhaps permanent change was already taking place about them.

For a long time, of course, there was no real unemployment. Workers replaced by one type of machine were soon re-employed tending newer inventions, and always the great frontier beckoned, absorbing the adventurous, the unemployed, the social and industrial misfits. Opportunities were still rich in the Middle West and in California, where agricultural lands and gold fields waited only for labor to convert them into the miraculous sources of wealth that were to help make this country great.

But gradually it was becoming evident to the American workman that these innocent looking contrivances were throwing men out of employment, and as a result labor unions grew up in an endeavor to combat the machine. Early seizing upon the idea of shorter working hours as a means of spreading out the available work, these unions even attempted to halt the Machine Age itself and to return to the system of hand labor which seemed in retrospect to be much more easily controllable. But in this they were inevitably to fail. The hand of time was not to be turned back, and progress—if it was progress—was not to be halted by the antagonism of any one class, however violent.

In the shortening of working hours, these labor unions made some actual advances, but even this was not enough, for the steady development of more and still more machines relentlessly raised the sum total of production ever higher, and hours of labor have been steadily decreasing, in a frantic attempt to hold the balance static. From sixteen hours a day to twelve, from twelve hours to eight, eight to seven, six, five, and the end not in sight. It would be a rash prophet who denies the possibility that this generation may live to see a two-hour day.

Now of course, the more machines that work for civilization, the greater the sum total of leisure available for society as a whole. That was obvious enough, and theoretically sound. The trouble was the laborer digging a ditch was extremely indifferent to society as a whole. What he was interested in was a little provision for the future, a little security for himself and his family, and all he could see was the ever-increasing danger that soon he would be replaced by machines—that his own survival was being jeopardized.

So to the laborer, with his insecure tenure on the necessities of life, the conditions that were making a new leisure possible were to him synonymous with unemployment, with all its attendant poverty and privation. His mind was too much concerned with the threat of "being out of work" for him to have any stomach for the rather vague possibilities of leisure—new or otherwise. It was inevitable then that there arose two distinct modes of thought with respect to leisure and unemployment.

One, remembering the plight of the laboring man, maintained that unemployment is not and cannot be true leisure. To them it appears as a circumstance, not a realization. It is a corollary of a social system out of balance, an enforced hiatus of honest work. They believe that this present leisure, enforced through lack of employment, is an accursed thing, and they agree with Dr. Fosdick that, "A museum is no substitute for bread, and a playground is not a roof against a winter sky." They hold tenaciously to the belief that until our economic system has provided an opportunity to earn daily sustenance and the most common appurtenances of living, there is small use in mouthing Utopian phrases about leisure in any true sense.

And on the other hand, there are those who point to the dictionary's definition of leisure as "free from occupation; spare; unoccupied; time available, as for some particular purpose." They claim that whatever disagreeable aspects unemployment may hold for the individual, it is still leisure, it is the raw stuff from which all art, all play, everything that makes life conscious of itself, must come.

And whether one inclines to this definition as touching on the center of the spirit of leisure or not, one must admit that the present widespread unemployment is a sign that our leisure problem, delayed here in America by expansion, by war, and by a period of inflation, has at last caught up to us, and demands solution. Some means must be found for more equitable distribution of employment, and it may be that we shall reach that fabulous two-hour day sooner than we think, for practically all recent plans to provide sufficient employment and to satisfy the rights of man for

13

food and shelter include features of employment limitation. They are the principles at the root of the National Recovery Administration regulations by code for restricted hours of labor—the forty-hour week and the thirty-hour week. It is well within the realm of possibility that Congress will eventually go so far as to crystallize these basic restrictions into definite law.

Whether or not one calls this unoccupied time leisure or unemployment, it is still contrary to the traditional American horror of idleness. Even the rich, formerly the only ones who could attain leisure, have found it in large measure incompatible with our pioneer instincts and with that spirit of "go-getting" so widely advertised as the essence and strength of our nation. These very men who acquired wealth would not or could not stop when their goal was attained. Giving themselves heart and soul to the life-long struggle for wealth, most of them never learned how to do anything else—certainly they never learned the high art of play. Midas-like, they had to watch everything they touched turn to gold and still more gold. They had to keep on being "go-getters," while their wives and daughters proved that they too were "go-getters" by playing frantically at the social game for power and prestige,

14

working at that occupation quite as hard and solemnly as their husbands and fathers labored at their business. To such as these leisure and its use as a constructive life force, whether individual or social, was bound to seem a wildly impractical and mythical theory not unlike the fairy tale of the treasure to be found at the end of the rain-bow. We were pioneers, and practical. We were hairy-chested and hard-fisted. And we didn't give a damn who knew it.

Poets and philosophers, to be sure, had already propounded alluring word pictures and idealistic conceptions of the delights of leisure. One might "sport with Amaryllis in the shade," or like the barefoot boy hark back to scenes of carefree youth before the knowledge of play was forgotten. Like the old tent-maker, one might cultivate the "loaf of bread, the jug of wine and thou, beside me in the wilderness," although in so doing he was very likely to run afoul of the local authorities. Or in the manner of the philosophers one might seek out that Nirvana of reflection and introspection, and religion. These were all elemental ideas, suited perhaps to a mood, but offering to most of us Americans no tangible or practicable recipe for a governing motive. It was too remote from us as a way of living, as a philosophy of life. As a

15

nation we did not care for poetic existence. As a nation, too, we have not cared for leisure.

So when leisure did come, we did a characteristic thing—we began to make excuses for it. With the early twentieth century, this leisure began to appear in appreciable quantities upon the American scene, and since it could not be harmonized with the traditional pioneer contempt for idleness, it had to be justified, somehow or other. It was at this point that leisure fell victim to the American belief that everything must have a *practical* use. We were still being pioneers. We were still being mindful of the hirsute adornment on our chests. So teachers and social leaders, seeking desperately to find a moral justification for leisure, found what they hoped for with the help of science, particularly with the help of the medical profession. It was a happy moment. The pioneer precepts, which seemed to have worked so well, would not have to be abandoned after all. Skillfully and very gradually the American was taught that leisure and play were not sinful if they could be classed under the head of recreation. As such they could be admitted to the category of acceptable and respectable occupations, since scientists, luckily, had found that neither brains nor bodies can work all the time and still retain full vigor and efficiency. The corollary was plain—one must play more in order to work better. So, complacently, our teachers and leaders told us to enjoy our leisure out of doors. They urged us to take up golf and other physical exercises not too violent, but—and here teacher and leader held up admonitory fingers—not because these things made us any happier but because they made us work better.

This health and efficiency slogan became the crowning manifestation of boom times after the World War. In 1926 it even attained Presidential recognition. Calvin Coolidge called a great national conference on outdoor recreation in Washington, and addressed it himself as spokesman of the new order. From every outdoor organization, from every corner of the United States, delegates attended it. Its sessions lasted a week, and thereafter the nation became officially "recreation conscious" and leisure-minded.

England was already ahead of us with a national conference on the leisure of the people held in 1919. Thus was signalized the acceptance of leisure not as an end in itself but as a valuable handmaiden of prosperity.

Alas for that conception! Those mad, glad days of Coolidge Prosperity and Hoover Bull Market were to fade as mists fade before the crash of 1929, and when prosperity dissolved, leisure was left stranded. Upon it all the evils of unemployment became saddled, and leisure, like other cogwheels of the social structure, seemed to have no fitting place. Some of our economic leaders, self-constituted as machinists for repair, seized hopefully upon the idea of trying to make leisure a stoker for the production power-plant. Put this little by-product back into the furnace, they reasoned, and it might be possible to make the flywheels turn fast enough to regain the momentum of those prosperous bygone times. Had not history good precedent for this? The little leisure that had been won in the past had created outlets for a flood of new products—the automobile, the movies, the radio, sports materials and countless others. Were not all these brought into existence by leisure and might it not happen again but on even a more Gargantuan scale? So newspapers and magazines burgeoned with glorious accounts of how leisure time could be devoted to ever greater consuming of products, and of how new products were to be discovered which would once more turn the wheels of a thousand factories.

So the makers of a nation's maxims issued new commands: "Free time is time for play," they said. "Play will necessitate spending, will create a demand for new playthings and new luxuries." The unemployed might be hired again, hours of work increased, until once more America would be a busy nation, using the unavoidable leisure to consume the things that only America could make. "Leisure," quoth these makers of mighty maxims, "leisure will raise the standards of living, and once raised, it will supply the means of its own support."

There were those impertinent enough to ask how people could spend more for luxuries when they could not even buy necessities. "Of what use to invent new toys," asked the impertinent ones, "when insufficient employment deprives men of means to earn the necessary margin?" But they were told that the depression was largely psychological, that it needed only a revitalized public interest—glorious phrase—in spending to bring out vast resources in savings and hoardings that would be adequate and more than adequate. The will to use credit would create the sources thereof. Installment buying and other inflationary schemes would tide us over. Leisure, which had been the handmaiden of prosperity, was now to be promoted to the position of major-domo in the ménage of progress and profit.

19

Of course, while this process of rebuilding a badly wobbling economic structure on the new basis of leisure was going on, and until it had accomplished that goal, leisure itself might appear to be a temporary burden. In such a state of affairs it would seem to place a duty on the more fortunate element of society to assist the less fortunate in alleviating enforced idleness. So new committees on leisure were organized. And this time they put forth plans for utilizing leisure with much the same motive as one might help flood-stricken China, or furnish pastimes for the feeble-minded, the maimed, and the blind.

Leisure, instead of being regarded as an opportunity, as an indispensable part of the stuff that human happiness is made of, was looked upon now as a burden, something one was unhappy to possess. What was to be done about it? Well, if leisure was to be treated as a temporary but salutary blight on the march of civilization, it should by all means be made as bearable as possible, and as constructive as possible. If by so doing we might stimulate spending so as to create a demand for more machine-made products and thus create more work, then this new leisure would lead us back to "Normalcy," and ring its own death-knell.

But unfortunately for the finest spun theories, the months of the depression slipped by without any noticeable progress toward speeding up the wheels of the economic engine through leisure. In the summer of 1933 the National Recreation Association made a survey to find out what the American people were really doing with their free time. Thousands of questionnaires were sent out and a report was based on approximately five thousand complete returns. From these it appeared quite clear that the very activities which necessitated spending were just the ones which were being most neglected. Old, obdurate human nature, it appeared, was again about its task of bringing to naught the well-laid plans of mice and men. More than ever people were patronizing libraries, reading newspapers, doing a thousand things about the home, but they were actually spending less than ever. The same questionnaire included statistics on unemployment and proved all to clearly that the kind of free time arising from unemployment led anywhere but towards the goal that wishful thinking had set—the goal of reviving production by means of leisure activities that called for the spending of money.

So the changing cycle of human attitudes toward leisure has gone on. The pioneer attitude of condemning leisure served its day. The conception of leisure as scarcely more than a health-builder aided nothing except the worship of production. Leisure as a stimulus to consumption has failed us. Even the later view of leisure as mere vacant time to be filled in as best one can offers small allurement to the active mind. Leisure as loafing, or leisure as a quest for poetic what-nots are alike unsatisfying. They may be sufficient for those strange anomalies that occur among us, but those of us who still have life to live, whether we believe it begins at forty or sixty, possess a desire—a desire that may be a deep-rooted instinct—to fill our hours with activity that is definite and creative. We want work or play, not vacant time.

What then remains? May leisure not possess some undiscovered social value and economic value in terms of human living? The fact that leisure cannot be successfully prostituted to end unemployment does not preclude an economic significance greater than any that has yet been discovered or officially announced. For leisure has a value far greater than this, far more fundamental than mere health building. And in spite of stacks of books and reams of articles to the contrary, it is much more than an incidental by-product to modern economic development.

THE DISCOVERY OF LEISURE

Leisure and human happiness—there is a significant and more than casual relationship between these two. It is only with leisure we are able to taste happiness. It is only with leisure that we are able to measure in any human terms at all the value of living.

But first we must disentangle the confusion between so-called economic standards of living and the social standard of a complete, happy and contented existence. Once that is done, leisure stands out as the great opportunity for America—an indispensable means of leavening our social fabric on a workable and a human basis.

II

AN ECONOMIC CHALLENGE

THE man who goes out to hunt a bear with dogs will probably return empty-handed if the dogs yield to the temptation to chase after the first rabbit, deer or raccoon. "Here is an attractive scent," say the dogs. "Something ought to be done about it." And off they go. The result may be diverting for the dogs, but it provides no trophies for the mighty hunter.

That is the way with us Americans. We possess a peculiar genius for nosing out problem after problem to challenge us, and with that same "something-ought-to-be-done-about-it" attitude, we lope eagerly off as if each problem were a major issue. For decades Europeans have smiled at us because of this very quality—we are a self-constituted nation of reformers, and one has only to read the platforms of many of our successful political candidates to realize that the American voter dearly loves his problem. Almost any sub-

24

ject will do, provided its appeal is dramatic enough to catch popular fancy. Very often the more absurd the problem, the more attention it commands. In recent years we have experienced delicious ecstasies of fear lest some sheet-clad gentleman of the Ku Klux Klan would find his way into the White House. We have devoted columns of public print and many hours of earnest barbershop conversation as to whether or not the British had perfected plans to seize and annex Chicago. Yes, we are very fond of our problems, we Americans.

So when we say that the New Leisure constitutes a challenge of free time that ought to be put to some good use, are we baying after a bear or just another rabbit? Obviously, if leisure is merely free time that somebody "ought to do something about," its challenge is decidedly minor; if, on the other hand, leisure may actually be a force capable of solving our vital economic problem, we may be after very big game indeed.

So it might be well to pause and ask ourselves this question: As human beings living among other human beings, what are our most vital problems; what forces must be overcome to attain our goal of the highest social-economic existence?

At the outset we must recognize that those very

terms, "economic" and "social" have long been confused by a maze of misapplication and abuse that serves as a formidable obstacle to clear thinking. Social factors, to be sure, concern themselves with those that are involved in man's existence and in his well-being as a member of an organized community—with that vast body of human phenomena that express themselves not as a function of any one particular person considered separately but as a member of some definite group. Economics, on the other hand, represents the field of daily bread and housing of individual and mass existence. But economics is not an individual matter, and its ultimate aim is essentially social. As our civilization grows more complex this interdependence between social and economic factors attains ever greater importance, so that sociologists are coming to use the inclusive term, "social-economic," in recognition of that close inter-relation. And in any large sense these two terms never could be separated.

Thus, the use of automobiles created an industry in America that was one of our most important economic factors and at the same time profoundly changed the social habits of almost our entire population. If the production of automobiles should suddenly cease, we would be forced to re-adjust the innumerable social devices and customs that have grown out of their use. Our social-economic structure would suffer more or less fundamental change. On the other hand, the power for change possessed by any one of these economic factors is itself a changing quantity. Thus, the widespread use of airplanes might conceivably so change our customs again that as an economic factor the automobile would become one with the livery stable of swiftly fading days.

Better to cut the gordian knot of what is a social and what an economic factor, and to say frankly that we cannot separate the two. We shall recognize that all economic factors possess social implications and that most, if not all, of our social factors bear direct economic significance; so we shall be content in the term "social-economic" as preserving our sense of close inter-relation between the two.

Now, as human beings existing in a so-called civilized system, our fundamental goal is a conceivable maximum of human satisfaction and contentment under a political state organized for its attainment. Satisfaction and contentment offer the only lubricant that can keep the wheels of the social machine running smoothly, and the contented state of mind is essentially the product of

27

but one condition—free and adequate opportunity for every man to develop his wishes and desires so long as these are not of an anti-social nature. To most of us life itself can be purchased at too dear a price, and that price is the relinquishment of the opportunity to express oneself—to seek out the satisfaction of one's desires.

A man's first desire may be for a good roof above his head and for three square meals a day. These are his minimum requirements, and society must afford him the opportunity of attaining them. If it does not, then for him and for the class he represents, society has no reason to exist, and should be destroyed to give place to another and more satisfying structure.

And yet this very task is one of the most difficult ones that man has put upon organized society. It can accomplish this purpose only by seeing to it that no one individual or group of individuals shall so abuse his opportunity as to endanger the opportunity of others. Moses, when he produced the tables on the Mount, sought to solve this problem through religious authority. The American Revolutionists hoped to find its answer without endangering the freedom of worship that was so important to them. Today Russia has determined to solve it, despite religion itself. And

28

despite the fact that for centuries this problem has been attacked from many angles of force and regulation and divine decree, the problem itself remains unsolved.

Of course, an honestly conceived attempt to found a perfect state in which no one individual or group of individuals could endanger the opportunities of another, is among the oldest activities of man. The desire to improve our social environment has ever been the dynamic impulse behind the evolution of economic doctrine—Utopia is one of man's oldest and most alluring dreams. Plato thought the answer was that magnificent scheme for social reconstruction, "The Republic," a society resting fundamentally upon a social division of labor, physically perfected by an elaborate plan of eugenics, and governed by the wisest members of the community. The Apostolic Christians played with the idea, as well as Aristotle, and Rousseau, in his *"Contrat Social,"* which was to have so deep an influence upon the founders of our own nation.

It was natural, then, that this credo should become the very basis for the original Constitution of the United States, whose authors naturally dealt first of all with the chief grievances of the people of their day, and in language which those people could best understand. They were men revolting from the much abused privileges and licenses of despotism, and they dreamed ardently of freedom and equality. To them it was the *sine qua non* of existence itself.

Now this very idea of human equality has an almost magic potency in touching the hearts of the masses. It is one of the necessary illusions of democracy. But just what does the phrase, "all men are created equal," really mean? The framers of this high-sounding sentiment were intelligent gentlemen of the upper classes and could not have been so obtuse as to fail to realize that all men are not and, short of an imaginary millennium, could not be equal in qualities of either body or mind.

In his "Historical Background of the New Deal," Professor Clifton R. Hall assures us that the framers of the Constitution certainly did not interpret this famous statement at its face value. The kind of equality these gentlemen had in mind was probably nothing more than the equality of equal opportunity for all. Every citizen of the new nation that was in the process of becoming the United States of America was entitled to an equal opportunity, free from the kind of privilege, class distinction and class slavery to which they had been subjected.

It was essentially the kind of equality that might be expected to exist in a new country, in a vast territory almost totally undeveloped as to natural resources. Land in those centuries before the Machine Age was the one chief asset. Benjamin Franklin was only just beginning to bottle up lightning in glass jars. There was no slightest realization of the empire of wealth electricity was later to create. Oil was a commodity used in small quantities for lubrication, and later for lamps. Steam had not yet made possible those great American railroad dynasties. But land—land was available and each man's power to wrest from it, by his own strength and that of his animals, the tangible assets he could force it to yield— grain, timber, minerals. And that land was free for the taking. All one had to do was move a little farther west. This was the great, glittering lure of America. This it was that brought equality within the scope of reality. This is what gave the Constitution its meaning.

Some cynic has defined tragedy as "a theory confronted by a fact," and as the years rolled on the fact of diminishing resources was to prove tragic to that stalwart theory of equality. All too clearly history has shown us how in due time the best land was all staked, the most usable forests were all claimed, the known mineral resources were brought under control of the far-sighted. Somehow in spite of the Constitution the more clever minds had succeeded in aggregating to themselves the lion's share of the fruits, and equal opportunity as a part of human daily living began to lose its meaning. But the phrase remained—it was too good a phrase to lose. Orators still ranted in the good old terms, school textbooks still glorified the term, but that magnificent ideal of the founders gradually shrank into the background, and with the development of the Machine Age it almost disappeared. It remained only as a kind of hope for fond mothers who could at least say that some day their new-born baby might become President.

Yet that deathless dream of equality still persisted in men's hearts. Professor Hall has shown how its original interpretation began to alter and to swing ever more powerfully in another direction—toward what we may term security rather than opportunity. And by the term, "security," men were thinking not in terms of protection against the daily hazards of theft or fire, but security in terms of livelihood—in the right to work, and in the duty of society to guarantee a

32

reward for labor that bore some satisfactory relationship to living conditions.

So in spite of old-fashioned textbooks, the bugaboo was no longer a King George, no longer the much abused privileges and licenses of a European despot, but the new manifestations of wealth and privileges right here at home.

The industrial condition of the United States had prevented the appearance of such a problem until within comparatively recent years. An ever moving frontier had led to a social stratification that was constantly changing, and the presence of free land and expanding markets gave ample opportunity for individual advancement. But when these easy avenues of opportunity became blocked, the struggle became acute. So it is in this light of struggling for security rather than for the earlier concept of equality that we must regard the attempted trust-busting of Theodore Roosevelt, The Strenuous, and thirty years later the measures of Franklin Roosevelt of 1933 and 1934.

So the picture had changed. Instead of equality of opportunity, the goal became equality in terms of equal right to secure a livelihood. But the chief obstacle in the path to attainment has always been difficult to surmount, and this obstacle is the fundamental inequality of human brains. Sooner or later brains, of a certain type, had always managed to accumulate property and wealth at the expense of those less gifted, and deprived them of their fundamental rights to equal security.

It is a problem inherent in all modern social-economic systems, and in common with other nations, the United States has tried innumerable ways to achieve some leveling process, with the hope that if it cannot eliminate the cause, it might at least mitigate the effects. Congress has enacted stringent legislation to these ends, but it cannot enact legislation to equalize the brain capacities of a hundred and twenty million citizens. Always sooner or later the brains keener than average have found some means of circumventing their best effort. And since in a state where money is power the keenest brains can be found where the most money is, it is an obvious assumption that cleverer men will be found devising means of evading laws than those engaged in making them. Government is usually at least one lap behind in this leveling, equalization effort. That this should be the case may be lamentable, but here we are not concerned with morals—only with the emphasis upon the problem offered by human inequality. And in these governmental efforts strictness of enforcement apparently does not answer the problem, for

34

this very strictness often deprives the economic system of a flexibility sorely needed in emergencies. It was exactly this difficulty that militated against the efficacy of our anti-trust laws.

Leveling processes—processes of equalization—many were tried and found wanting. Sliding scale income taxes were imposed in the hope of making the rich bear the burden of government and thereby gaining a partial redistribution of wealth that better brains had accumulated at the expense of others. The trouble was that super-brains, owned or employed by accumulated wealth always found some loop-hole to avoid the intended weight of the tax burden or to pass it on to the public, who use the products which these superior brains have managed to control. From income tax to inheritance tax the history of all our legislation is filled with such cases. It bristles with interpretative emergency regulations and with stop-gap attempts. Even poor old average John Doe is beginning to realize that the flamboyant promises of politicians to free him from the tax burden and place it upon the shoulders of the rich do not seem to materialize except in campaign oratory and in the highly imaginative pages of the *Congressional Record*. "Soak the Rich" was a popular sport until it became apparent that the weapon used was a boomerang.

But all undaunted and even more actively than ever before our government has taken up again the cudgels of economic security for Mr. and Mrs. John Doe. An inevitable depression had emphasized the need. Our government now undertakes to tax the rich on incomes and inheritance in the hope that this time a plan can be devised that will work. It undertakes to apportion employment so that work shall be spread out more evenly among the greatest possible number of persons. It strives to level freedom to the individual security scale. In these attempts it may temporarily succeed, but one must remember that against any permanent success there is aligned the strongest force of human nature—the fundamental inequality of brains. This we have not changed, nor have we changed the fact that always keener brains are crying out for power and prestige, are grasping for tangible recognition of their superiority, and for the kind of adulation that attaches to it.

It is incontrovertible that the human urge to exercise superiority is as fundamental to the race as the demand for equality itself. It is a psychological paradox, and it is certainly the source of

36

a great portion of human discord. The human need to win accepted forms of public recognition is as natural to mankind as is the human demand for security. Both are fundamental demands for human self-expression, but upon different planes. And always these two elemental forces are continually at variance, just as much now as under European governments of the past. One prevents the attainment of the other, and no social system which fails to give recognition to this truth and to make provision for it can permanently endure.

It is the inability to prevent keener and sharper minds from upsetting the balance of security that constitutes the essence of every indictment of our individualistic or capitalistic system. It is a primary cause of that class struggle which, when unchecked, often culminates in terrorism and bloodshed. It will always culminate in bloodshed so long as any one class is forced to live the life of a machine while working and at other times the life of a beast. It has been maintained that under the capitalistic system no effective solution of this conflict is possible. Where then, shall one look? Shall we look to communism, which claims to have solved the problem through the foundation of a presumably benign but absolute and despotic oligarchy and after a great deal of bloodshed and arbitrary elimination of individuals?

But communism, as demonstrated in Russia to-day, can offer to Americans very limited grounds for a comparative study. Its value to us as a social-economic laboratory is impaired by the fact that Russia is still in that state of almost totally unde-veloped natural resources which the United States occupied before our Civil War. In Russia there need be no real over-production problem for a long time. There would appear to be ample outlet for the keener brains developing their resources without the actual need of preying upon brains less gifted or able to defend themselves. For so long as there exists ample opportunity, in terms of undeveloped resources, there is much less temp-tation for the individual to exert his superiority at the expense of others.

Look as we may, then, we can find no golden key to the solution of our problems, and we are forced to the conclusion that in the rest of the world there is no readily adaptable formula in practice that can aid us. If we must find a means of eliminating this bitter conflict between the principle of a fair measure of economic security for all and this innate human desire for power, we must discover it for ourselves and apply it to whatever social system we are developing here in the United States.

True, there exist throughout the world small groups of people among whom the inequality of brains is so weak that as a social factor it is non-existent. These people have no outstanding leaders and little individual or mass incentive to "improve their lot." They have not been led out into the confusing complexities of modern civilization by self-elected apostles of progress, and lacking ambition in any particular degree, they are contented and often among the happiest people in the world. It is this fact which social experimenters either resent or seem incapable of understanding.

But these groups are generally more or less isolated and constitute communities that for one reason or another have rejected modern education. The poor farmers of China, the unspoiled Navajo Indians of the remote desert and outlying portions of the United States—these are examples.

But these, too, however fortunate their lot, cannot serve us as guides. They have no value as precedents, for we cannot duplicate circumstances such as theirs, even if we would. Nor can we set them as a goal for ourselves. For good or for ill the people of the United States possess a restless urge, an unquenchable desire—a craving—for what we term "success"—more perhaps than other nations. And the reason may lie in the preponderant inheritance of the American pioneer instinct, for in spite of his many short-comings, the pioneer was either a go-getter in his time, or faded from the picture by methods more or less violent.

True, we are not all descendants of the original pioneers, yet most of us do come from a mixed stock in which the pioneer instinct was strong, and all of us have been imbued from earliest childhood with what are essentially pioneer ideals. Even those later waves of immigration that built up our population were largely composed of men and women who were not content with what life offered them at home. They were eager to take a chance on the future. They were willing to alter their whole lives in the hope of attaining some better lot. In essence, if not in common understanding, they too were pioneers. They were men and women who maintained the right to exercise their ability to the full and to profit by these abilities to the utmost, and from all these pioneer-minded immigrants we Americans take our inheritance of social ideals. Our public school system and all our education has been built upon the adulation of successful pioneers and of individual achievement. It is directed toward the wor-

40

ship of superiority, of "go-getting," and of acquisitive ability. And—we may as well admit it, for others have admitted it for us—we inherit also, as part of those pioneer ideals, a lawlessness, a sense of "might makes right," and a worship of power for its own sake, irrespective of the ends to which that power is directed. Our pioneer inheritance may not have made us a better people, but it certainly made us a more active and acquisitive one.

So long as our free and undeveloped natural resources offered equal opportunity for all, just so long was this widespread American pioneer spirit an economic asset. "Bigger and better" was our motto—"Bigger" especially. Then came the end of the frontier. Opportunity in terms of land and other resources was no longer open to all, and those very qualities that had once been our strength began now to be our undoing. Those creative pioneering instincts, once they lacked constructive fields for expression, turned predatory. The instinct itself survived and strove now to gain by winning the bounty of the earth from others. A constantly more complex system of economic distribution was built up wherein the profits poured into the hands of the middlemen who had used their brains to create a seemingly logical

41

place for themselves, and little by little wealth was being diverted into their hands rather than into the hands of the real producers. Today our farm problem is the outcome of just such a process, and we find ourselves faced with the necessity of re-simplifying a delicately adjusted and extremely complex organism.

With changing environment the pioneer instinct, diverted from its conquest of an undeveloped empire, turns now to despoil all weaker abilities and to feed upon them. Mediocre brains fall victim to shrewder brains in the competition until, by the survival of the fittest, security is lost not only to the original producer, but to many more who feel it to be their inalienable right to exist in comfort and security. Such a process goes on between chain stores and the smaller merchants just as definitely as between the middleman and the farmer—and for the same cause.

But we have not yet ended with the undesirable aspects of this thwarted pioneer instinct. Once obstructed of an outlet in legitimate channels, it manifests itself in warped and unsocial short-cuts, and under the stress of greatly restrictive environment turns criminal. Even in the days of actual pioneering this was true, and many for lack of mental or physical equipment to compete with

42

their fellows on the social plane, turned bandits, horse thieves, cattle rustlers. These were the organized gangsters of their era, and the present-day wave of criminality takes its origin from circumstances that are not fundamentally different. It is the same ingredient turned to a different channel. Human craving for recognition, for success, power, the very qualities that made our pioneers, the very qualities that brought successive waves of immigration to our shores—these are responsible for the bad as well as for the good. The instincts that made us great, now, under changed circumstances and environment, operate for our destruction. The pioneer type of mind, turned to criminal activity, deprives our lives of security, and the mania for the accumulation of wealth—another perversion of the pioneer instinct—takes away the security of our livelihood. In their essence the two situations are close kin. The criminal makes use of guns, the money-mad makes use of brains—the purpose and result are the same—the victim is robbed, whatever the method.

So, until we can find some new means to control this thwarted, perverted human instinct, we must admit our inability to achieve even an approximately perfect economic state. We cannot wholly

43

depend on law to do this. We have already seen that laws and regulations exist presumed to be the bulwark of principles laid down by the Constitution and as a means of obtaining the equality that mankind eternally seeks. Through law we have built up a complexity of prohibitions designed to protect us, but we have not been protected. Although the machinery of law grinds slowly, sooner or later we manage to legislate against each new undesirable manifestation of this pioneer spirit. But always that pioneer spirit crops out in some new, unpredictable form equally undesirable, and as a result we have an ever-increasing flood of restrictive legislation that threatens to turn our civilization into a government of "Thou shalt not."

Already the nation has suffered from one great prohibitory experiment which failed so clearly that it had to be undone, and it seems hardly probable that the Federal Government will ever again legislate against the drinking of alcohol. For whatever else it did, the Eighteenth Amendment proved that laws and prohibitions can serve only to supplement and define a general willingness on the part of the people as a whole to cooperate and to give force and meaning to its edict. Laws can punish individuals who run contrary to

44

generally accepted sentiments, but prohibitory laws alone cannot defeat any fundamental human instinct, and the craving of superiority over others or the desire to exercise that superiority for the satisfaction and supposed happiness of the possessor is one of the earliest characteristics of man.

What, then, can be done with a force as fundamental and as indestructible as this? It cannot be destroyed, but can it not be used to serve useful social ends? Psychologists and sociologists both agree that in dealing with instincts there is only one method that will give permanent results—to direct these instincts into socially and psychologically satisfying channels.

Today there still exist channels capable of using this excess of pioneer urge, this excess of superior mentality which otherwise is destined to burn up its energy in unfairly handicapped struggles or else to steal the rights of security from those less well equipped. And these channels, these new fields, are to be found in a new conception of the use of leisure and in a new attitude toward the use of leisure activities and occupations wherein life, centering upon doing for its own sake, rather than upon production alone, will not only aid us in guaranteeing the opportunity for every man to attain security, but will at the same

45

time widen the fields to attainment of those other human desires that make for happiness and social contentment.

As a sufficient goal for modern civilization, security is not enough. Even if security can be forcibly controlled and equalized among every citizen by social regulations, it can only be done at the expense of our restless, creative will to do. It could not absorb our surplus activities. We must have opportunity, with all its potentialities for mental and physical exertion. Opportunity is as indispensable, from the standpoint of human contentment as is security to the physical existence. It is opportunity that we must rediscover and make free to all—opportunity that is social in its operation, that has full regard for all security rights and—most important of all—opportunity that demands from each one of us the best that we can give.

III

LEISURE ACCEPTS THE CHALLENGE

INNUMERABLE phases of modern family life serve
to illustrate the imperious demand of our creative
instincts for opportunity to express themselves.
They exist from infancy and may, in fact, be
more exacting at that time than in later adulthood, but at no time are they very easily dealt
with. Every well educated parent, for example,
knows that although the rule of "don't" must be
invoked at times, there is usually a better way of
avoiding domestic discord. The entire trend of
modern education is based on the realization that
this restless creative instinct of the child—of
which the pioneering instinct itself is a part—
must be given full play. It cannot be simply ruled
out at the risk of repression. It must be directed
into constructive channels, channels that are social
in their results and not harmful to others. For in
its very essence education is a work of liberation
and of vitalization—and for modern children we

47

find the answer in the right type of play. Teach Junior an acceptable activity that will absorb all his interest, and automatically you have removed the danger of his putting fly-paper on the cat's paws, tinting Mother's frock with jam, making a football of Father's favorite hat, or engaging in any of that apparently inexhaustible multitude of anti-social activities that the unoccupied child is driven to by utter boredom and curiosity. The right type of creative play not only keeps the child contented, but lays the foundation for greater future mastery in the art of living itself.

Now if we apply these same principles to the essentially similar but wider field of adulthood, is it illogical to assume that a rightly directed use of adult leisure and of interest outside of work is capable of supplying a vital factor in solving our fundamental social-economic problem? The two endeavors are essentially the same, and however distasteful the fact may be to our carefully bolstered egos, modern psychology is increasingly emphasizing the fact that personality problems in the adult are the direct outgrowth of unsolved or illy solved problems of the child. Psychiatrists again and again point out the close relation that the gangsters and clever crooks of today bear to the Juniors of yesterday who got in the jam. The misfits of today are suffering from just this lack of creative outlets—outlets that would have had greater social survival value than clever swindles, or taking a racketeering competitor for a ride. Former Secretary of War Dwight F. Davis relates that in his experience as Park Commissioner in St. Louis he found fewer cases of delinquency among boys wherever playgrounds were installed, and that in such neighborhoods the boys possessed keen conceptions of sporting ethics.

So with youth and adulthood alike, the object to be kept ever in view is furnishing legitimate and social outlets for the human creative instinct, which otherwise is so often diverted by our modern intensive civilization into channels that are essentially predatory. In a word, we must once more offer opportunity to each perplexed and baffled pilgrim in this complex, modern world of ours.

So leisure becomes not merely a problem of free time which "somebody ought to do something about," but far more than that—it becomes part of our problem of free and abundant living. Our exploration of the question of leisure thus bids fair to lead us not after the rabbit, but on the trail of the bear itself. It confronts us as a truly economic and social challenge which we cannot well

49

afford to disregard, for the right use of leisure possesses the potentialities of a solvent to inequality and is itself a method for surmounting the barrier that has stood in the path of adequate social-economic development.

Leisure, then, wisely directed, would seem to provide a freedom from the intolerable burden of life's economic inequalities. It holds out to us a realistic approach to what had almost seemed the unattainable end of a Utopian rainbow—the opportunity for full expression and contentment under the existing scheme of things.

Of course, leisure cannot hope to accomplish these things without direction. Its mere existence is not enough. Neither can leisure hope to bring about any millennium, for leisure, after all, is in itself the by-product of a security that it helps to protect, and without reasonable progress in guaranteeing security by regulation and law, there can be no true leisure in the first place. But it is this very security that has been provided in greater abundance with the passing years, and we have good reason to assume that the war against unemployment will be carried on with a reasonable degree of success—that the first great step toward economic reconstruction will be made. Once this is accomplished, the challenge of the economic and social potentialities of leisure loom large and alluring before us.

Now, if every form of leisure occupations had equal social value and were a source of equal satisfaction, the problem would be essentially simpler than it actually is, and one of the difficulties lies in the proper valuation of its many diverse forms.

For the number of adult occupations, interests, or avocations, is legion. They run the gamut of human possibilities, from the most trivial kind of satisfaction and notoriety to the highest means for winning respect, honor, and the kind of public acclaim that affords to its recipients a profound and satisfying sense of power. Of the former especially there is no end. Each week the news reels portray the delighted if somewhat vacant smiles of the latest champion of every type of achievement that imagination and modern publicity can conceive—pie-eating, hitch-hiking, marathon dancing, hog-calling, flag-pole sitting—the list is endless, and rather depressing. Strangely enough, the rewards of these naïve achievements are truly comparable with those attainable through the accumulation of wealth. It is even debatable if Mr. One-Eye Connolly, for example, would exchange the notoriety attendant upon his position as No. 1

American gate-crasher for the anonymous security of some un-headlined millionaire.

The difficulty in rendering the potentialities of leisure of service to mankind lies not so much in discovering an interest as in the public attitude toward those interests. For those old-fashioned school masters and arbiters of fashion whom we mentioned before in passing, have taught many generations of us to look down on all occupations that do not pay well in currency of the realm. We have, in the jargon of the day, been made "currency minded." The result is that many a young man with musical or artistic leanings has, by a false popular dictum that such pursuits were unmanly and un-American, been deliberately discouraged from a pursuit that might have given his life meaning and satisfaction. Many an amateur beginner at sailboat or radio design, or stamp collecting, has been told as soon as he passed childhood not to waste time on such profitless pursuits, but rather to bend all his efforts to emulate some big banker hero or other Napoleon of industry. And although for the moment the laurel crowns of many of the big business champions of yesterday lie deep in mud and mire, it might not take long, given proper incentive and in spite of bitter betrayals, to uplift to public pedestals a new dynasty of such heroes.

Perhaps what we actually need is a revaluation of life's values—a re-classing of the purposes of living under the changed environment that the past few years have forced upon us. For these values have been swiftly changing, and it is not too late to start now and through education and wisely directed precept, to obtain a re-estimate of their significance in modern life. Well, what are these values? Wealth is perhaps the answer that comes first to mind, and yet wealth beyond the temporary satisfaction of actual physical wants usually begets more wants, and results merely in an accumulation of "things," whose power to bring pleasure is essentially transitory. When all is said, the truest and most lasting satisfaction is in the activity of creation, in the winning of a struggle, in the doing, and the making, in the thrill of attainment, in the honor and adulation afforded to real accomplishment.

And if achievement is the surest means to human happiness, it is also the only measure thereof. It is the achievement that we honor, and to the extent that wealth is a single type of achievement, we afford it the honor that is its due. In the past we have afforded it actually more

53

honor than its due, for the simple reason that it is easily measured, that it has been the most publicized and is the logical outcome of a typically "go-getter" ideal. Yet, as other opportunities for achievement are broadened, interest tends to draw away from the accumulation of wealth toward other roads that lead to success, respect, and honor. And this, too, is in the service of greater social stability, since in giving honor to other forms of success than the accumulation of wealth the competitive stress on our economic structure is modified, and the age-old conflict between the urge for superiority and the right for security loses something of its bitter competitive force.

Now at this point the reader may assume that like so many sermonizers we are leading up to the age-old plea for participation in politics and similar well recognized forms of public service. The writer hastens to give assurance that he has no such intention. He maintains rather that public service, while well suited to certain types of mentalities, offers no hope of opportunity on sufficiently broad scale to afford an adequate field for many of our people. Public service is to be highly commended, but it should be regarded merely as one form of activity among countless others. Toward the great city of universal opportunity that

54

we hope to build it is one highway, and only one. As such it may be left for later consideration when we take up in greater detail the fields of leisure.

Some of these fields, of course, are already dear to the heart of the average American, for as a nation we accept and give honor to a multitude of forms of physical achievement. We throng in ever-increasing numbers to college football games, where we honor the star players with a fervid adulation almost worthy of a better cause. We extend headlines, film footage, and unlimited glory to the "Sultan of Swat," the man who thrills us by knocking a home run to order. We dial the radio and tune in on a boxing match, even if we are reluctant to attend in person, and the name of a pugilistic champion comes as readily to the lips of the Wall Street magnate as to the boy who sells him his evening paper. Our interest in the pugilistic art is reflected in the fact that the Dempsey-Tunney championship bout in Philadelphia claimed an attendance of 120,000 persons, and the return match in Chicago totaled in gross receipts over two and a half million dollars. These are primarily athletic pursuits that appeal to the eternal small boy within us.

There is good reason for the great popularity of such contests. For by the psychological process of substitution we gain the supreme pleasure of imagining ourselves the hero. We ourselves are out there in the ring, battering a mighty antagonist into submission. We ourselves are carrying the ball for our alma mater while the stands rock with cheers. We are no longer harassed, everyday toilers, no longer one obscure taxpayer among countless others. For the time being we are living gloriously, and the very impossibility of attaining to these heights in actual reality is part of its appeal to us—is the basis for the recreational value which the experience itself affords.

As a matter of fact, very few of us make any serious attempt to emulate these heroes. Of necessity we regard their world as a thing apart, as something interesting, exciting, and somehow satisfying to observe. It is a release from our own lives, a form of vicarious entertainment. So this attendance at professional sports must be regarded from the angle of leisure occupations more as a psychological release than as a primary outlet for any surplus ambition, or for any realistic means of affording expression to our creative instincts.

And herein lies the danger of that type of leisure in which we ourselves are not actually participants but take part only by substituting for reality the stuff that day-dreams are made of. For this substitution destroys what real education should give. A vital function of education, after all, is to give us an increasing sense of reality, an ability to cope with the real environment about us, and has nothing to do with those multitudinous means of flight into pleasantly alluring byways that have no real existence.

Yet it is hard to realize the enormous sums that are being spent in this country on commercialized leisure. As a nation we devote as many dollars to commercialized leisure as we do to food, and we invest in its enterprise more than in any one thing except land itself. Every day more than twenty million people in this country pay admission to motion picture theaters, and for two hours live the vicarious life of hero or heroine. Eighty thousand people will see a Yale-Harvard football game, paying over one million dollars to witness twenty-two athletic gentlemen disputing the geographical location of a pigskin. The cost of equipping, training and conditioning each one of these twenty-two collegiate Tarzans has been estimated at no less than twenty-five thousand dollars. Each day twenty million people tune in on the radio throughout the United States, where, between impassioned appeals to use this or that particular product sponsored by the company that may happen to be then broadcasting, these twenty millions experience varying types of entertainment in which they have no active participation.

As we approach the types of entertainment that do call for active participation we come closer to those activities affording satisfaction to creative impulses. Such a sport as golf offers this type of amusement, since actual participation is made possible to all of its two million followers. It comes closer to being a nationally and popularly indulged sport than the majority of other games more highly professionalized, and as such possesses greater social value. It, too, has its honored heroes, most of them at least technically amateurs, and to the amateurs who follow it, golf often becomes quite as absorbing as their own active money-making business. So golf has legitimately consumed much individual and personal ambition, and comes close to furnishing a type of worth-while leisure-time activity among recognized outdoor sports. But of course, here too the personal equation is all important. To you golf may be nothing but a passing hobby, to me it may possess no appeal at all, while to our neighbor it may be the one activity he lives for.

Well, after all, there are many other fields toward which we can turn. In the pursuit of constructive leisure we need not even confine ourselves to games, although many of them require an intensive mental concentration no less than physical effort. Fortunately there is literally a host of activities with diverse appeals to different types of minds, and to the entire gamut of varying abilities. And when once we accept the dictum that the only essential difference between work and play is the presence or absence of the element of necessity, we must logically admit that practically any human occupation may become an absorbing leisure time activity provided it is not pursued primarily for commercial reasons. In leisure the motive is the important thing. It is the fact that the occupation is being pursued for its own sake, freely, and in the absence of all necessity. Thus, men and women otherwise employed to win a livelihood, may devote their surplus energies to raising vegetables or flowers, or even enter into the more extensive pursuit of agriculture. In this intimate contact with the soil there exists for many of us a satisfaction and a creative thrill that appeals to something even older and deeper than the pioneer instinct itself—a return to the great Mother Earth that nurtured us during the untold thousands of years before we became city dwellers.

Unquestionably the food garden movement sup-

59

ported during the World War, accomplished far more in terms of the morale of the gardeners than in actual amount of food produced, large as that was. For these food gardens offered to restless, harassed minds a desperately needed diversion into channels sufficiently constructive to forestall any possible psychological outbreak that might have been inimical to the nation's immediate task of winning the war. During the recent depression this same principle has again called into service the creation of thrift gardens for the unemployed. Federal and state governments alike gave support to the community gardens idea, not so much because of the value of the food per se, but because they offered opportunity for occupying minds and physical energy, and acted as a stop-gap to any potential upsetting of the already threatened economic régime. They gave a much needed respite in which to attempt essential steps of recovery.

But to name all the various amateur occupations capable of absorbing man's constructive and creative needs would fill the pages of a bulky and extensive catalogue. Engineering hobbies alone extend from more or less expert model building all the way up the scale to full-sized construction of the real thing. The writer recalls one of the most successful vocal teachers in the United States who, on his estate in Maine, has built three miles of model railroad tracks where run all the most modern of streamline types of locomotive, reduced to model size.

There are hobbies pertaining to art, and their number is legion—painting, sculpture, architecture, design, and scores of others. The wide and fertile field of literature is open and ready to absorb the best mental powers of all who will give to it their "new leisure" time. Music, in any of its protean forms, offers a lifetime of intensive application, to be followed with an absorbing seriousness hitherto attained by professionals alone.

But the list is endless, and in each one of these fields there is outlet for an infinity of man's creative power and ambition. Interests and ability grow, and the value of amateur effort becomes more widely recognized as the numbers of amateurs increase, while the effort itself, with increasing appreciation, reaches ever higher planes. And if in such games as golf, amateur and professional standards have existed successfully side by side, may one not expect parallel development elsewhere?

In the field of the dramatic arts we have already found it, for there amateur participation grows yearly, and encouraged by leading professionals themselves, attains to higher and higher amateur standards.

Now of course, there are other fields for leisure time development which have no professional parallels at all. In some of them the money-making aspects are actually dependent upon amateur participation. These, for the most part are of a class appealing directly to the unmodified, undiverted pioneer instinct. Camping, hunting, fishing, exploration, and other closely allied activities belong here. Each one of them is worthy of far greater public support than has ever been accorded in the past, since the opportunity for their continued enjoyment depends upon the preservation and management of natural resources according to wise and thoroughly far-sighted plans. For in this appeal to the primordial man in us, we are dealing with very deep and fundamental things, with instincts that must have outlet or become perverse, with needs whose exigencies lie beyond our conscious ken. And each year opportunities for the enjoyment of these activities become less—each year the wilder portions of this continent are becoming increasingly invaded by the ubiquitous filling station and the fumes of carbon monoxide. So it may be well to sound this note of warning in passing—that we need here not merely protection against selfish commercial destruction, but equally against too ardent road building, too much "improvement," destined to destroy the appeal of these natural areas to our sense of pioneering by rendering them too easy to be capable of any satisfaction.

Although the "New Leisure," is being enforced first of all upon factory workers and others of the laboring class through unemployment, it is no less necessary that a similar control be applied to the capitalist class, particularly to that stratum which possess the best brains and ability. For we have already suggested that if men of more than ordinary brains cannot be persuaded to divert at least a part of their abilities from the main task of gaining wealth, they will, in spite of all the well meant laws of the universe, find some means to take wealth from the less gifted and to endanger the delicate balance whose purpose is economic security for all.

The recognition of this social axiom supplies the very reason for applying the "New Leisure" to brain workers as well as laborers—to the leaders as well as to the rank and file. For the very brains and the very leadership that yesterday were used for the accumulation of wealth must tomorrow be applied to the direction of new leisure pursuits, to the organization of new activities that are to be substituted for the long working hours of the past.

This activity in organizing the "New Leisure" will give to these leaders that sense of power so necessary for the contentment of the ego and at the same time will provide direction to leisure itself.

For after all, leisure will not take care of itself —not for the laboring man nor for any who lack the qualities of dynamic leadership. Like every other widespread movement, the new leisure demands wise supervision and control, whether you call it paternalism or not. Laws and agreements creating shorter working hours solve no social problem with any permanence, and even if the distribution of work could be so successfully organized as to insure a job for every able man, there would still exist labor troubles, arguments about pay, competition between capital and labor. As a matter of fact, it is already too clear that increasing leisure gives increasing opportunity to reflect upon injustice, real or imagined, increasing time for demagogism, and for its concomitants.

And left to itself, we have no good reason to believe that among the laboring classes the new leisure would follow other than the time-worn, vicarious channels of the past. Athletic contests, professionally manned and promoted, would thrive. Movies and other devices that depend for their recreational value on psychological substitution would be sought out in increasing numbers as leisure itself increased. Savings would be exchanged for admission tickets—so long as the savings lasted. There would be no new development, merely a widening of old channels, with no reason to hope that this sort of satisfaction could better absorb the energies of sons and daughters of restless immigrants and more restless pioneers in the future than it has in the past.

Endless processions of laborers' automobiles would line the highways, not only on Sunday but on workless week days, and we would see an extension of these futile, aimless wanderings vaguely dictated by a psychological desire to exchange present environment for another, wanderings limited only by the savings available for gasoline. And although all this may sound like a golden prospect for the automobile maker, the tire producer, and the oil refiner, it is not a process capable of indefinite expansion, and it is certainly not in line with the social solution we are seeking, for this very wandering is itself symptomatic. It is a groping after the very things wisely directed leisure will supply—the satisfaction of the creative will to do. No, leisure must be directed toward other pursuits than the spending of money. Leisure must have nothing to do with money as its primary aim, or it ceases to be leisure.

The unplanned, uncoördinated direction of leisure time into still other channels may have no other effect than making prosperous the manufacturer of some new product or the promoter of some new idea. And what chance will do for the new leisure of the laboring classes, no one can foretell. Some of the results may be constructive. Some may stimulate industry and create new demands for labor that will in turn reduce idle hours. But it is all a muddling, undirected process, without definite plan and leading to no particular goal.

So it would appear both unsatisfactory and insufficient to leave future leisure to chance and to the old, well-worn and for the most part commercialized recreational channels. It becomes just as important to plan a new standard of life's values for laboring classes and for the super-gifted groups of the upper strata alike. One needs the other. For the attainment of complete social satisfaction, both groups, both classes of instinct and abilities represented by these groups, are necessary. Education must be directed to this end. Leisure activities must be developed not just as pleasant time con-

66

sumers or even health builders, desirable as these may be, but they must possess the added goal of supplying definite outlets for excess energies and for competitive instincts. For many they must furnish a prime purpose of existence itself. Machine-tending labor gives no purpose to life, and the more monotonous and repetitive the task, the greater the need to supply a purposeful goal somewhere else. The more a man's working hours become a mere tending of machines, the greater his need for some realistic, creative outlet in his time of leisure. And although such labor will not and cannot create love for the mechanical tasks of life, it can be compensated for, and the guardian of the machine, while giving a fair modicum of attention and service to the demands of his livelihood, will make his real life and find his real satisfactions outside the work itself.

And so perhaps from the vantage of this new viewpoint we can begin to plan both direction and goal for the new leisure. We shall not exclude recognized recreational activities, but on the basis of a well planned organization we shall add new ones. To accomplish all this we shall call on the best talents and the best brains our nation affords, knowing that in carrying out this very task we are already proving the value of this new leisure. The task itself will be a heavy one. It will be necessary to classify interests and abilities appealing to various groups of individuals and to recognize that such a classification will be entirely separate and distinct from the classifications of regular employment. These classifications will bear no relationship to the tasks of workday existence. The leisure interests and latent abilities of the steel worker or coal miner may run the gamut between literature, music, cabinet making, painting, farming, and a host of others.

But the direction in which these interests run will not be so easy to discover, since our steel worker or coal miner himself does not know—he has had no opportunity to find out. Examination of correspondence courses taken by laborers reveals a woeful failure to choose wisely, and reflects more than anything else the glittering lure of high-powered advertising. So once again the idea of leaving to chance or to private exploitation the direction of leisure development proves definitely wanting. As a matter of fact, in spite of our best efforts, it is going to be difficult to even scratch the surface so far as the present adult generation is concerned.

Properly directed, the scope of leisure activities is limitless. Innumerable fields now occupied solely

68

by professionals, lend themselves excellently well to amateur participation. The example of model-building clubs for those mechanically inclined comes to mind, and already we have magazines devoted exclusively to this activity. Community groups under adequate direction, aided by the stimulation offered by museums and guided by the supervision of professionals will be called into being wherever there are enough persons sufficiently interested, and this, too, for its successful outcome, will require careful planning and management.

Already we have outstanding examples of Nature Clubs, Camping, Hiking and Trail Clubs, for those who love the wild places for their own sake or to satisfy the old inherited instinct for direct pioneering in contact with the unmodified, unspoiled, forces of nature. Under the new leisure these clubs will be encouraged and their number multiplied many times. Camera and photographic clubs offer still another classification for similar hobbies, and all these great group activities provide opportunity for healthful and constructive competition, while national federations of clubs of similar purpose offer, on a scale broad enough to be satisfying to the most demanding, the satisfactions that come from individual honors and rewards.

There are a number of indoor activities that include collectors' clubs of various scope and kinds. Among these postage stamp collecting has become very popular among adults. The collection of stamps, or philately, as it is called in its advanced form, provides a good example of the creative brain work called forth by collecting. Many a high-powered business man with philately as his hobby has written scientific tomes on research and discovery in this field. And there are many strange and varied examples of scientific clubs scattered throughout the length and breadth of the land. Nor are these to be disposed of as simply aggregations of freaks, for they serve as examples of thousands of other similar groupings for leisure-time pursuit which, if given a little encouragement, a little assurance of public support, will develop into health giving and constructive growth.

Indeed, America's new opportunity, its almost untouched store of mental resources which are ready to take the place of our old material resources so lavishly exploited, is to be found in the hobbies of today and tomorrow. We may laugh at some of them. Some we may condemn as a waste of time, but they are not, in the deepest sense, to be laughed at—not one of them. Nor is one of them a waste so long as it offers to the interested participant a chance to exercise part of his excess power, part of his desire for invention, for research, for construction, so long as it affords him the opportunity to pit his own powers against the unknown and the undiscovered. Perhaps the difficulty is in the term "hobby," for it seems to indicate something of childish origin, some not-to-be-seriously-considered vestigial remnant of our infancy. Very well, then, let us use some other name. Call them interests or avocations, or what you will, for under whatever name the benefit to be derived from them will be just as fundamental, just as satisfying. And that benefit lies not in any careless attitude of the bored dilettante, but in the very self-absorbing seriousness of the pursuit itself.

Whatever term we use, let us at least agree that the scope shall be wholly non-exclusive. Let it be so broad as to include public service and religion —both capable of becoming absorbing leisure-time activities of transcendant value, that need no special pleading from the moral standpoint.

Carefully examined, the moral aspect is never absent from any leisure-time activity, but on the other hand, its presence greatly widens the horizons of those once narrowly conceived fields of public and social service. Perhaps, as a partial result of the old puritanic attitude, the term "recreation" has come to possess connotations of purposeless play, activities ordinarily supposed to be quite separate from and possibly at variance with a hastily conceived idealism. Yet this conception is not to be found in the term "recreation" itself, for surely the ideas of creation and recreation extend far beyond the narrow limitations of a selfish hedonism. Actually the very opposite is true. The idealism required for intelligent recreational leadership calls for the highest form of public service —a form that need not suffer even in comparison with religious ministry itself.

Recreation leadership, sorely needed as it is, deserves to become, and under the new leisure is probably destined to become one of the most honorable of professions. And if the wise use of the new leisure is to be taught, this comparatively new profession might well retain thousands upon its payroll, and at the same time, like other forms of public service, offer opportunity for every honestly competent amateur who may choose this field as his own particular interest or hobby, regardless of what may be his actual source of livelihood.

On the subject of public service in its restricted sense of political leadership much has been written about and sermonized over. So much so that we mention it only after a discussion of other forms of practical hobbies. Most of what has been said by others is so obviously true that little can be gained by reiteration. It seems to boil down to the terse fact that many persons have qualifications for public service and many others have not. As an attack upon the entire problem of new leisure, public service has no wider application than agriculture or any other pursuit. Yet it may be well to emphasize one feature—while politics offers a most necessary and obvious form of service to the state or the social body, equally real and valuable service to social progress may be rendered in many other ways. Educational leadership—is not that a valuable social service? Or any practical recreational leadership, whether it be technical, scientific, or legal? These occupations partake very essentially of a public service nature where they are pursued not for private profit, but on the social basis—as an amateur, the term amateur being used in contradistinction to professional, not with any connotation of ineffectiveness or dilettantism.

From the standpoint of psychic well-being the best service, after all, is that which is performed for the love of the doing, for the gratification of an ideal, for the honor that is awarded to excellence and merit in social advancement. And in this

73

sense service to the public reaps its own reward,
for even when human idealism fails to supply sufficient incentive—as it often does—the winning
of the plaudits of the multitude supplies an ever
practical and satisfying goal.

There are no rewards and honors more easily
won than through various kinds of really useful
social leadership. Up to the present at least, there
has been all too little competition. No field of
pioneering presents more fertile soil and fewer obstacles than the field of non-political public service. There is little doubt that this type of reward
and honor will be the lot of the leaders promoting
wide use of the new leisure. The old puritanic days
have passed when recreational activities were aus-
terely frowned upon. The days of the great commercial struggle, when everything not "big business" was despised—these too have passed. Today
recreational leadership need not hang its head in
the presence of either puritanic bigotry or industrial arrogance. Today the promoters of outdoor
recreational developments, sports, wild land management, game bird and game animal supervision,
are being called into the councils of the great. Tomorrow the new leaders and promoters of a hundred other hobbies and interests will sit beside
them, taking their own necessary place in the great

social economy of human welfare, voicing their essential opinion in those matters which govern the affairs of a nation. How can it be otherwise? For in a very real sense, it is these leaders, these guardians of the new leisure who will aid us to find life itself, to surmount the mere mechanics of living and attain the Elysian heights of unobstructed opportunity for all.

PART TWO

SOME SOCIAL IMPLICATIONS

IV

THE NEW LEISURE AND THE SOIL

MAN needs an antagonist, both for work and for play. From the time of Eden itself the greatest of his antagonists have been the forces of nature, and all his victories, all his essential progress, man has won from a struggle with these elemental forces. Like the mythical Grecian hero who each time he was thrown to earth arose ten times stronger than before, man has drawn his deepest strength from the earth, from the soil he tills, from the rocks he forces to yield up their store. This struggle between man and nature still goes on, and ever she gives him a hard-fought battle. She is a worthy antagonist. But the compensations are direct and visible. They lie in the golden grain of the harvest, in the gleam of metals brought up to the light of day, in the long, straight-grained logs wrested from the forest. Such successes as these are very tangible. They are

79

fruits that can be grasped and eaten. They are an embodiment of creation.

Since all these things are yielded by the great sustaining power of the soil, or by the mysterious processes of earth's hidden alchemy, it is in no way strange that throughout all time and in every portion of the world, primitive people have worshiped the Earth Mother as the giver of strength, the great co-creatress of life. And deeper than any tribal superstition there lies behind this universal conception a fundamental truth—a truth that can be ignored only on penalty of much suffering.

Some measure of direct contact with the forces of nature, some visible and comprehensible act of creation in coöperation with the soil, is part of the heritage and inalienable right of every man. Indeed the tremendous development of cities, resulting from modern industrial expansion, has proved this contact with nature to be more than a right—it is a necessity. Deprive man of intimate relationship with the soil or some equivalent, and his bodily powers, as well as his spiritual and mental fiber, weaken and decay. Surrounded by steel, concrete, asphalt, and glass, doing the same meaningless, repetitive job day after day, with no feeling of creating something in its entirety, the worker becomes ill-adjusted, unhappy and unstable. Over his life descends a sense of impotence that is not the lot of one who lives in contact with the soil. For, though the city worker's capacity may be no greater, the tiller of the soil acquires a feeling of power from making the earth yield to his desires. As a consequence, for all his grumblings and complaints, he is really and fundamentally happier and better balanced than the city man from whom these creative contacts are denied. Literally and figuratively, those who live beyond the reach of cement pavements have their feet on the ground.

Throughout the ages farmers and tillers of the soil have been the backbone of democracy. Always agrarian people have been the easiest to control, because they have been invariably the most contented. Nor is the Agrarian Revolt of recent years in our Middle West a denial of this axiom, but rather an outgrowth of commercial marketing complexities that have been grafted onto agrarian principles by the so-called march of civilization. The farmer himself had fallen victim to that spirit of go-getting, and, when the opportunity of expanding frontiers and limitless acres was shut off from him, he sought out new opportunity in applying what were euphemistically called "modern methods" to the land he already owned. These "modern methods" are the source of his present troubles. One-crop farming, encouraged by greedy middlemen; over-extension, stimulated by short-sighted bankers; a general attempt to superimpose upon agriculture systems that applied to machine production and manufacturing—all these were modern methods. The trouble was that they didn't help the farmers.

What is now called subsistence agriculture is a return to the age-old principles of producing a direct living, in whole or in part, from the soil. It has absolutely nothing to do with Machine Age specialization or large-scale production undertaken to decrease unit expense. Neither have its rewards, its effects upon the tiller of the soil, anything in common with industrialism. Because agriculture embodies hard work, it builds character, tenacity, ruggedness, and individualism. Because it envisions the changing seasons and nature's moods of friendliness, of beauty and creation, it feeds the very soul of man and raises up his eyes to the infinite possibilities of wider horizons, until he is no longer a cog of man-created machines, but a living power at one with creation itself.

Just as agriculture is being called upon to make its contributions in the readjustment of human relations, so the nation's forests must play their part in the program of social rehabilitation. Municipal forests will be increasingly called upon to aid in the liberalization and development of community life, and to serve as a stabilizer of agriculture itself. For part-time employment in forest, farm woodlot, or in municipal forest, is serving the double purpose of an outlet for creative endeavor in direct contact with the soil, and, in addition, providing an added means of livelihood leading to a greater fullness of life itself. As part of the New Deal, the forests of the nation became one of the important vehicles for absorbing unemployment and putting the youth of the country at wholesome, satisfying tasks. So, in the coming era of the New Leisure, the forests, too, in common with their blood sister, agriculture, will help provide those fundamental satisfactions that spring from contact with Mother Earth.

To assume that we can bring about a universal exodus from the city to the farm and forest, and reëstablish in any literal sense the old pioneer methods of living is, of course, not even to be hoped for. Long before Rousseau's time, theorists had urged a "return to nature," with varying results, but never with success. For civilization, as a whole, has progressed too far and become too complex to be abruptly turned back by any intellectual gesture. As a matter of fact, there is grave danger in too enthusiastic pressing of the idea of a return to the soil as a complete panacea for social ills. In the first place, the art or science of farming is a very exacting pursuit, in which none can succeed without training and experience; in the second place, we must not lose sight of what today amounts almost to an axiom —properly managed, and on good soil, small-scale farming can yield ample food for the farmer, but it can seldom produce the complete ingredients for our present standard of civilization.

While we are today confronted with the necessity of returning in some measure, at least, to the soil and of utilizing it as a foundation for rebuilding society on a firmer, happier basis, many will seek this soil contact without sacrificing any of the city's conveniences. For these a sufficient sense of recreating may be obtained through cultivating a garden, or merely through ready access to fields and woods. The need will be an individual need, varying as one's adaptability to urban conditions varies.

Because man possesses a brain and an intelligence which refuses to stagnate, he must add something to elementary existence that will utilize and challenge his brain powers. And, conversely—man being a paradoxical animal—he finds it unsatisfactory to live by brain alone, so that one whose work entails intense mental application will usually seek his recreation in outlets that require almost pure physical effort. Probably this is the reason why the best examples of successful simple-life communities can be found where these two extremes are combined. Simple living, it would seem, thrives best when hand in hand with the pursuit of art, literature, music, or one of the sciences. Art colonies based on the simple life, such as that at Woodstock, Vermont, are examples. These colonies, in the final analysis, are but working communities of what we shall presently refer to as subsistence homesteads, pursuing on the one hand a profession eventually intended to be the means of livelihood, but drawing recreational strength from the soil.

This recreation with the soil as its source is one of the goals of what is now called the Subsistence Homestead Plan. Into it both Federal Government and the states are pouring millions of dollars to enable men and women with agricultural leanings to live where they can produce crops for their own consumption and thus contribute leisure time toward their own immediate support. It is the old, Rousseaunian, "back to the soil" idea, sweetened with the prospects of subsidy.

And, since these Subsistence Homesteads give every prospect of being publicized as a coming influential factor in our social-economic life, it might be interesting here to dwell briefly on the philosophy of their purpose and on the mechanics of their organization.

Subsistence Homesteads, in the first place, are generally promoted by Federal, state, or private organizations, which acquire abandoned farm land and attempt to colonize it with people believed capable of so managing the land as to obtain for their own consumption food crops commensurate with their efforts. Now, the term "homestead" implies that it should be a home, and it should also imply ownership by the person actually living there. To bring about this ownership, public or social aid has generally been required in the past and will undoubtedly be required in the future. This does not mean that the land need be given outright to the family cultivating it, but by small payments or the performance of certain acts, and by the efficient management of the homestead itself they shall eventually win title to it.

It is of little practical importance to the Subsistence Homestead idea whether the land is marginal or sub-marginal in comparison with land used for producing market crops. The economic factor of markets may be entirely disregarded, and the question resolves itself solely into whether or not the land is good enough to be cultivated and to produce varied rotational crops under reasonable management. This means that, as a matter of practical necessity, the choice is limited to fairly good land.

But, although the Subsistence Homesteader farms purely for his own subsistence, and the sale of his produce is no part of the essence of the project, it is probably neither wise nor necessary to prohibit him from selling his excess products, if he desires. The very term "subsistence" implies food, and must include vegetables, meat, flour, sugar, as well as other staples. Therefore, to obtain a full subsistence, there should be a sufficient excess of some products to permit exchange. It is surely out of the question to suppose that the modern farmer will grind his own flour, nor can he, in most sections of the country, produce sugar, salt, pepper and other necessities. He may, to be sure, keep chickens, cows, and pigs, but, on the other hand, he may prefer to specialize in a few commodities and trade through the stores or directly with customers on a cash basis. He may

87

raise sheep or goats, but neither he nor his wife will dress in homespuns. He will need machinery, which must be bought.

The Subsistence Homestead is designed to contribute all that it can toward the requirements of living and in every practical way. But for the rest, security must depend upon the outside job.

As a matter of fact, this inability of the homestead to guarantee of itself the security every individual should have, has been recognized by the Federal Government in its Subsistence Homestead Plan. Under this project the homesteader depends upon leisure-time farming or its equivalent not for livelihood itself, but for a greater abundance. Security of livelihood must come first from wages, salaries, or savings, and, recognizing this, the Government requires, before granting homestead applications, that the applicant himself be possessed of some income. The amount of this income varies in different localities, but whether the homesteader lives in Alabama or West Virginia, it must be sufficient to insure a certain satisfactory standard of modern living.

This need for a supplemental job or income is the primary element essential to the success of any subsistence homestead plan, whether undertaken by government or by private organizations. Only when the means of making a living are assured from some other source can the main purpose of the plan be successfully carried out. The practicability of subsistence homesteads will, in the long run, depend upon migrations of manufacturing industries from cities to semi-rural communities where agriculture can be practiced during the leisure time of workers. According to the proponents of these subsistence homesteads, such a migration is inevitable; but here one trespasses upon the dangerous ground of prophecy.

In any event, the plan itself can not be put into effect more rapidly than such migration permits. So it would seem that subsistence homesteads, at best, will certainly not be available immediately on any impressive scale. Important as the idea may be in New Leisure planning, it is doubtful that the development will, for many years at least, be of service to any large proportion of our population.

Although the creative outlet of the subsistence homesteads seems at present to be restricted to comparatively small numbers and to special conditions, there exists another outlet which is easily available to practically all city dwellers—the Civic Gardens movement. This Civic Gardens idea is essentially an adaptation of the War Garden

89

movement, a movement which antedated the homestead plan by many years, and may indeed have been its forerunner. Fundamentally, there is little difference between the two.

In the Civic Gardens plan, the plots for cultivation are not necessarily owned or lived on by the family. They are made available at one or more central locations, where specific plots are assigned to each participant. The abundance of vacant land suitable for gardening in close proximity to towns or small cities makes this idea eminently practical. Transportation to the garden area is, of course, necessary, but this is scarcely more difficult than transportation from the home to office or factory. The essential difference lies in ownership, with the Civic Gardens idea partaking more of the nature of tenant farming than of actual land owning. From the psychological standpoint, there is always a practical advantage in a man's actually owning the land he tills and in having it as his home.

The element of public investment in a Civic Gardens plan is usually not so large as for subsistence homesteads. Local projects are generally promoted by private social organizations, or by public community services organized for social welfare. In Lakewood, New Jersey, where the plan is most extensively operated, the greater part of the land was either donated or secured by the Community Service at nominal rental. The paternalistic element lay in furnishing without charge seeds, fertilizers, insecticides, and so forth, to participating individuals and groups. The money for this purpose was raised partly by contributions from private individuals, and partly by use of public relief funds.

The Lakewood plan is also distinctive as an example of effective coöperative management. The Community Service Committee in charge divided the participants into groups, with local self-government, so that the greatest possible element of individuality and freedom was preserved, while, at the same time, authority as to what constituted the proper care of land was vested in the gardeners themselves. This scheme was most effective.

And, although the source of financial management is undoubtedly paternalistic, it is possible to maintain the financial advantages of this system, together with a high standard of group action and individual freedom. The importance of this becomes apparent, when one realizes that practically all attempts to organize relations between the New Leisure and the soil are social experiments requiring participation by the public, especially in its financial aspects. There is grave danger that where public participation goes so far beyond financing as to constitute public interference, the whole social value of the movement may be lost.

Civic or community gardens have become widespread. They are found in nearly every state as an outgrowth of the war against unemployment, and even in the dry lands of the Far West we find successfully operating projects. In these dry countries it is necessary to furnish irrigation water rights, under some organized irrigation project, or a pumping plant. In Albuquerque, New Mexico, a nineteen-acre tract operated for the relief of the unemployed furnishes an example of such a plan far removed from Eastern centers of population. In 1933 this tract furnished nearly twenty-five hundred dollars' worth of garden truck, and produced, in addition, three thousand pounds of shelled corn for distribution. Instruction in the preserving and canning of vegetables is here, as elsewhere, an integral part of the plan, for the value of agricultural products is, of course, enhanced by the ability to keep them over the winter.

Now, it must be realized that many community garden projects, just as this one at Albuquerque, were really undertaken not as New Leisure projects, but for the value of the sustenance and possibilities of relief for the needy. Work on community gardens organized for this purpose is allocated much the same as any other work created for the unemployed, but with this difference: The community garden idea, besides being an activity of proved practical value, has an advantage over most other types of created employment, in that, as in the case of the War Gardens, contact with the soil, even on such a diminutive scale, possesses the power to bring sorely needed solace to distraught and harried minds.

More than once in the course of these chapters we have pointed out that there can be wide difference between unemployment and leisure, and one of the great values of civic and community garden work organized to deal with the problem of unemployment lies in the fact that it can readily be made to serve leisure activities when the immediate demand for relief subsides.

Now, at this point it may be objected that in urging the growing of farm and forest products as part of the New Leisure, we are contradicting our own theory and transgressing a law of economics. For, presumably, we are suggesting leisure activities, all of which have at least as a secondary purpose diminishing the strain of competition for a livelihood. At the same time, we are proposing amateur entry into a field of activity where there is said to be already too much competition and overdevelopment.

It may be well to pause and consider this question carefully and honestly, for it will arise again, in varying degree, with respect to amateur participation in other activities to which professionals look for their security of livelihood. And, since agriculture is, perhaps, the sorest of all points in our seemingly chaotic economic system, it offers an excellent test.

Now, the amateur who produces food or anything else as an amateur, does so primarily for his own pleasure, and, to a secondary degree for his own consumption. In so doing, he ceases, in part at least, to be a consumer of similar professionally produced goods, but by this very fact he increases just so much his own purchasing power with respect to still other goods. The home gardener who grows his own beans and apparently deprives the grocer and farmer of a sale, will undoubtedly take that money which he would otherwise have spent in purchasing beans, and buy something else. Hoarding is a crime against any economic system, but spending is not. Suppose, therefore, that over the whole season our amateur gardener saves enough money on those home-grown beans to buy a radio. His purchase of a radio helps the radio industry, and a thriving industry tends to give employment to more persons, who, in turn, can buy beans which otherwise they might have been unable to afford. So the trade one grocer loses another gains, and in the last analysis the farmer will sell no fewer beans than he sold before; and, in light of the knowledge that many people are always close to starvation because they can not buy food, it would seem futile to contend that the farmer will be injured in any way by amateur gardening.

But, conversely, does the man who gains leisure-time pleasure and satisfaction from building a radio deprive the radio manufacturer of a sale? Follow out the process to its conclusion. By building his own radio, the amateur will either save money for some other purpose, or he was no prospect for a radio purchase in the first place. To be sure, he may use the money he saved from buying a radio, and with it buy fresh strawberries for breakfast, when ordinarily his family would go strawberry-less. But the farmer gets the money for the strawberries, and with this may buy a radio that otherwise he would not have been able to afford. The process, then, is a complete circle, and at no part of its revolution has anyone really suffered.

Of course, if we were urging all the people of the United States to take up gardening or radio-building to the exclusion of other amateur leisure-time occupations, it might work disastrous hardships upon the farmer or the radio builder, the grocer or the radio retailer. This, of course, is far from our intention, and, even if one of those hysterical waves of faddism that sometimes sweeps the nation should actually bring it to pass, the resulting hardship would be only temporary, and not nearly so serious as professional calamity howlers would have us suppose. Indeed, the history of mechanical development in the United States is the history of one displacement after another—all progress is displacement. The music box and the parlor organ were elbowed out by the phonograph, and the phonograph, after tremendous mushroom growth, was suddenly made obsolete by the radio. Now the radio trembles in turn before the real or fancied advent of television. Yet somehow or other even the most abrupt cases of obsolescence seem to cause no permanent difficulties. Always there seem to be factors that modify and mitigate the total effect.

So, in the case of subsistence production, the

gross effects would be modified first of all by the fact that such production guarantees the consumption of its products—it does not threaten to throw them into an overproduction discard. In the second place, any apparent upset to the economic system would be tremendously diminished by the well-known inefficiency of the average amateur as compared with the professional. By and large, the majority of our amateur gardeners would probably succeed in whetting their vegetable appetites without producing enough, either in variety or quantity, to satisfy them. The grocers and truck farmers will still have a very tidy business. As a matter of actual fact, this was well demonstrated during the much publicized War Gardens movement of 1917–1919, when it was estimated that the total home consumption of all truck garden products increased by just about the amount that amateur gardens had added to it. And, as a parallel development, many radio manufacturers are agreed that the home radio-building craze has stimulated the demand of the American public for more and better radios than most amateurs can ever hope to construct.

And, even if, in the last analysis, these modifying tendencies should fail to balance the situation, and a few farmers or radio producers should be

97

forced out of business, the ultimate prosperity of the nation would in nowise be endangered. For it is the success of many industries and many occupations, rather than of any single one, that governs our national prosperity. Scientific progress is constantly rendering obsolete factories and businesses, processes and materials. It has always done so. It is a continuing motif that runs as a never-ending theme throughout the great symphony of economic progress. It is a part of the wear and tear of civilization's march. And, finally, amateur production, guaranteeing as it does a consumption of the excess products it creates, actually tends to raise the standards of living. It can not lower them.

So the charges of inconsistency or false economic reasoning can be safely disregarded in our proposal to make use of the New Leisure in productive amateur enterprise. Secure in the knowledge that the conception is tenable, we shall adhere to our original thesis. A diversion of excess ambition and a desire for honor and success away from money making fields and into leisure-time activities will render easier of attainment the control of men and machines in accordance with the American Constitution and the ideals of its framers. Leisure activities will serve to overcome those obstacles in the path to assuring every citizen the right to earn a suitable livelihood.

But that is not all. Our ultimate objective is far greater than that—it is to render life not merely tolerable, but also more interesting, more satisfying, and, therefore, contented. Our ultimate aim has to do with the deepest fountains of our physical and spiritual being, for it seeks to restore the strength and moral fiber of every one of us by affording to the most humble his inalienable right to contact with creation. Direct and intimate contact with nature herself— that is the old and proved way, that is the way of the pioneers. That is why agriculture, the direct coöperation of man and soil, bulks with such tremendous importance among New Leisure activities.

V

THE NEW LEISURE AND NATURE

MAN has never quite outgrown his early environment. Throughout his racial history he remains essentially an animal, akin to hundreds of others that have never risen to the heights of conquering the world about them. This racial memory that links civilized man of today with those early Cro-Magnon ancestors of a dim remote past still has its own dynamic effect upon our present mode of living, rendering us intolerant of the rapidly multiplying complexities of modern life. For simplified living, after all, carries with it the seed of happiness and contentment on a basis that is firmer and more lasting than the thrill of new inventions and artificial excitement can ever be. So it is that equally with agriculture man renews his nature contacts by camping, hunting, fishing, mountain climbing, and practically all forms of nature study in the open—activities that offer their varying appeal, and requiring the development of those pioneer virtues, independence and resourcefulness.

These pursuits offer little or no conflict with professionally organized fields, nor do they contribute in any important degree to means of sustenance or to standards of living. They are generally seasonal in their application, and their great recreative value to man lies in their very emphasis upon the simplification of life and upon the elementary principles of existence so often lost sight of in civilized living.

So fundamental, so universal is this need to return to a simpler life that, with the aid of our enormously increased transportation facilities, it has created a profoundly significant trend in modern recreation. Forced forward by an urgent popular demand, there has been a rapid expansion of outdoor recreation facilities within the past fifteen years. Within that period more than two-thirds of the present state parks and forests have been established, and appropriations for administering and improving the National Park system have increased from approximately one million to twelve million dollars.

In the past few years there has also been a remarkable development in organized hiking. Although there have been some hiking and mountaineering clubs of long standing, the real growth in this activity has come since the War. With it there has been a tremendous development in hiking trails, notably the development of the Appalachian Trail, now—except for one small link—completed all the way from Maine to Georgia. Thousands of feeder trails join this route, and along its length there have sprung up many groups whose leisure will in large measure be devoted to hiking. There is a close affiliation and often an identity between these hiking clubs and nature clubs. The majority of hikers are interested in the flora and fauna and geology of the region through which they hike, and most nature club members must hike to see the things in which they are interested. With additional leisure there is opportunity to form more of these groups among like-minded individuals and to revive and extend the activities of the groups now in existence.

Yet, despite the annually increasing efforts of states and Federal Government to meet the public clamor for more outdoor recreation facilities, the demand has only been very inadequately met, and the problem of providing an outdoor environment suitable for leisure activities available to a large portion of the population is difficult.

For it assumes, in the first place, a broad plan

of land management that our nation, as a whole, has never possessed. True, wild lands suitable for game and fish are not lacking, but in most of our states appropriate administration is still woefully inadequate. And for all this there is no good reason—no reason at all other than our own lack of foresight and our failure to become good stewards of our wild life heritage. For, when we consider that more than half the area of such populous states as Massachusetts, New York, New Jersey, and Pennsylvania has been adjudged unsuitable for any farming or industrial purpose, and that this area is exclusive of all the large cities and centers of population, the potential availability of wild land as such becomes evident. It is wild land, true, but it is not suitable for outdoor recreation; nor is it a suitable environment for wild life. It is land covered with over-exploited forests, scarred and burned-over wastes, interspersed with streams polluted by the wasteful processes of commerce, unfit for humans to drink or fish to live in.

This thoughtless wastage that renders so much of our so-called wild lands unfit for recreation is illegal, even under our present laws, and, regardless of regulation or restriction, it is totally unnecessary. Factory pollution along our streams, al-

103

though chemical in its nature, is an outgrowth of the careless principles of pioneer development, when Americans believed that natural resources were so limitless as to be capable of any kind of abuse. It was a direct echo of the old "doctrine of inexhaustibility" that still persists—inexhaustible forests, inexhaustible wild life, inexhaustible carrier pigeons. It was pure waste that no European country could have been rich enough to tolerate. Were our nation less blessed with raw materials, it would be necessary to reclaim much that is now simply sent through sewer pipes into rivers and streams. And even today engineers tell us that much of this acid and chemical waste could be converted at a profit into valuable products.

Factory and chemical waste, of course, are not the only sources of river pollution. Much of it is caused by the sewage of towns and cities, in spite of the fact that modern engineering is capable of converting it into harmless and even useful products. In most of our eastern states, the law provides due process for eliminating sewage pollution, but so large is the offending portion of the population, and so general the custom, these laws are not enforced.

There is an additional reason. Sewage disposal plants cost money—a great deal of money—and the wastefulness of politicians has so depleted the credit of many an urban community that extremely few are in any position to finance even much needed public works. Recently, in New Jersey, a group of public-spirited citizens obtained from the Reconstruction Finance Corporation promises of Federal funds for sewage disposal plants provided the communities benefiting from them would enact legislation to charge householders and factory owners for sewage service on the basis of their water consumption. In this way the disposal projects would be rendered self-liquidating; but, unfortunately—as might have been foreseen—the political leaders were unwilling to cooperate. They felt that because sewage disposal had always appeared to be a free service, they would lose political support by urging direct payment in proportion to the service rendered.

So, although the potentialities for outdoor recreation in this country remain greater than in almost any nation in the world, our wild land assets continue to be needlessly abused and spoiled. We abuse them in a multitude of ways, and often by the very steps taken to develop them, and here, too, the pioneer point of view is an important factor. For it is this very pioneer idea of "conquering" the wilderness, converting it to our artificial

105

standards of civilization, that is destructive of any really far-sighted recreational use. The craze for over-development, for rendering things easy, has claimed as its victims many a trout stream, many a quiet secluded lake. Wherever there remains some beautiful natural area where fish and game are still able to thrive because man can not gain access to it in an hour's easy motoring, we build smooth, easy-graded highways and draw into it all the restless fishermen and hunters from far away. It is an increasingly destructive process, for the very men and women for whom these areas are ruined today must go still farther afield tomorrow in their search for the outdoor life, since concentration upon newly developed wild places soon ruins them, rendering them unfit for the very purposes that gave reason for their development.

So, in one or two ways we have been signally successful in bringing ruin to our natural areas— either we destroy their usefulness by wasteful exploitation, or by over-development we deprive them of the very charm that gives them their allure.

Now, our "progressive" fish and game commissions throughout the states strive to maintain artificial fishing and hunting grounds, and make these inadequate areas serve ten times the number of people that the natural increase of fish and game could possibly support. In artificial hatcheries they raise trout to a size suitable for the angler, then dump them full grown into some one or more of our few available unpolluted streams. The public is invited to hook them out in a mad scramble, a concerted mass attack upon the fish that possesses no remote resemblance to the gentle art Izaak Walton wrote of so lovingly. Glance at this or that little bridge on any early morning of the open season and see the fishermen lined up shoulder to shoulder on every square foot of ground, whipping the water's surface with countless lines, while the comfortable cars in which they came a hundred miles or more are parked row on row above the pool that their owners infest. Then wait a few weeks. Hardly a fish will remain alive.

Sport? You can call it that, perhaps, but it has woefully little in common with the unspoiled environment of real sport and with the restful, contemplative mood that angling in its old natural conditions was wont to bestow upon the fisherman.

The same sorry truth applies to game. In hunting, as well as in fishing, the "sport" has been made so easy for the automobile owner that he

flocks in ever-increasing numbers from his distant
home, until the concentration of sportsmen not
only defeats the end of the sport itself, but each
year results in the end of dozens of hunters. Our
commissions hatch a thousand pheasants and lib-
erate them like so many domestic barn fowl to
wait for the day when the deliberately promoted
"hunting" instinct of the public may be turned
loose upon them in an orgy of wholesale destruction. Whoever believes this an exaggeration
should turn to the Government's estimates of
hunting and fishing licenses issued each year. At
least seven million licensed sportsmen yearly turn
to our woods and streams in search of game, and
this total does not include a single one of the
many anonymous hunters and fishermen who deliberately break the game laws, who hunt without
license, or who enjoy these sports unhampered in
states where game laws are only feebly enforced.
Altogether, the total number of both lawful and
illegal hunters and fishermen in the United States
can not be less than ten million people.

Of course, it is impossible wholly to deny that
this form of intensive, "mob-scene" sport does not
supply some modicum of valuable recreational
end. It certainly does. Its very popularity is proof
enough of the human craving to return to nature

and to satisfy pioneer-inherited restlessness in the open—a craving, incidentally, that leads American sportsmen each year to spend more than five million dollars for fishing tackle and equipment. But its artificial standards are leading sportsmen after false gods and are gradually destroying much of the fundamental benefit that comes from contact with nature. In the first place, the very ease that we strive so eagerly to introduce deprives the participants of their right to fulfill an urgent subconscious need. To make anything popular by the simple device of artificially removing all its difficulties is, in the long run, to destroy most of its value. For it removes that sense of accomplishment, that sense of victory over an antagonist, without which we humans derive scant satisfaction from our activities.

In still another phase of outdoor life the disastrous effects of this passion to remove all difficulties is equally apparent. It is the conversion of the crude roadside camp of yesterday into the comfortable, rented cabins of today. This is almost typical of the entire camping movement. Equipment is no longer carried by the camper, but is provided by the renters of luxuriantly furnished cabins, and it is not unusual for fishing and hunting lodges and other types of camps to advertise among their attractions such Spartan necessities as electricity, steam heat, plumbing, radio. Even in the more remote places the attempt is made to approximate urban conditions as closely as possible, and, although true camp life of the traditional sort still exists, it is much rarer than the modern radio-steam-heat sort of thing which is developing into little more than a country roadside hotel.

What happens to the pioneer instinct when confronted with these enervating conditions? It has coped with no difficulty, conquered no obstacles, and has actually been rebuffed in its attempt to seek new life at the breast of Mother Earth. It is a frustrating process, and a half hour spent in any one of our great commercialized modern camps will convince any dispassionate observer that the campers themselves have not found the indefinable something they came in search of.

Of course, the proponents of this type of recreational management, whether in the specialized fields of hunting and fishing or in the more general phases, believe that, in removing all difficulties that lie in the way of contact with nature, they are aiding the many as opposed to the few. They are, in the phrase of the later Roosevelt, "democratizing recreation." The question is at least debatable, and, for the present, they may be right.

The trouble lies in the implied corollary that this is the only way to aid the many to enjoy the out-of-doors and in the obvious fact that fish and game commissions alone cannot solve our land use problem. They cannot cope with forest destruction, stream pollution, with the senseless drainage of swamp areas where native wildfowl breed, or with the often abused rights of private property. The moral here would seem to be that in this great field of recreational development there lie ahead almost unlimited possibilities for wise leadership, for well-planned programs of land use, for far-sighted control.

Already there are two schools of thought regarding the methods which recreational development should follow. One of them has long been established, and takes its historical background from the American Revolution itself. Revolting against the narrow feudal restrictions of the mother country, wherein fish and game belonged only to the nobles, Americans have decreed that all game belongs to the public, irrespective of the ownership of the land—no one may exercise prior rights to hunting and fishing. Under such a system land owners have no vital personal interest in advancing fish and game protection or propagation. They may post their land against trespass, but they may not in any way aggregate to themselves the wild life that makes a home there. And, because the public is owner of the game in fee simple, it becomes a public duty to take whatever measures are necessary for game management and game protection.

If private land owners desire to exclude others from their property and are able to enforce such exclusion, it follows that the problem of providing any substantial areas for public recreation necessitates public purchase and control. New York, Pennsylvania, and several other states that are most prosperous and progressive have accordingly undertaken more or less extensive land purchase plans, but these, like all other paternalistic schemes, are a function of government, depending upon large appropriations of money. If we are to solve our recreational problem to the degree of making available enough wild land and returning it to the condition of natural balance it once possessed, it is going to be necessary to extend this development to many other states, and to a degree far beyond present limitations.

Recently we have come to recognize the great potential recreational value of our National Forests —a value which may be greater than any purely economic value—and, as a result of the Forest

Service's liberal policy toward recreation, there has been an enormous increase in the number of visitors to the National Forests. These forests, however, are largely limited to the principal mountain regions, and by far the greatest number is in the West, far removed from the great massed centers of population. As a matter of fact, out of a total of one hundred forty-seven National Forests in this country, only nineteen are located east of the Mississippi River.

This National Forest development possesses the great advantage of a centralized administration, whereby it avoids many of the mistakes and pitfalls of the states, nearly all of which have different land policies, and are greatly handicapped by lack of funds. The Government, too, has been far-sighted enough to initiate a policy of setting aside wilderness areas in these National Forests, in the hope of maintaining intact their natural conditions, and to preserve the delicate balance that is inevitably destroyed, once it is made accessible by smooth and easy highways. And, were it not for the fact that practically all the public land units are already honeycombed by small private ownerships, it might be possible to exercise a successful policy of management throughout. But, under present conditions, the apparent Constitutional

113

right of any citizen to live where he pleases has done much to complicate and render extremely difficult the ultimate attainment of any broadly planned land policy.

Besides the National Forests, we have the great National Park system, whose areas are also located largely in the West. These National Parks represent one of the finest examples of recreational land management, and, thanks to the championship of the press, have been kept almost entirely free from private and political exploitation. Each year millions of people visit these great Federal areas, and the few state parks that have been set up on similar principles are constantly being made the objects of wider recreational use.

The problem of whether or not to extend the public ownership of land so vital to recreational development as a national policy is influenced by many factors. The first of these is at present an economic one. It arises in connection with a proposal to remove from competitive production submarginal lands no longer farmed, or precariously operated in competition with an adequate supply of better agricultural lands. These areas, if purchased, would become public property suitable for recreational development. In a parallel way, areas of abandoned forest land have become a vital economic problem throughout the once well-forested regions. The original forests have been exploited or otherwise destroyed, and the private owner, feeling that no cash value remains, has failed to pay the taxes over a period of years, with the result that the states are deprived of a sorely needed revenue.

There has been no satisfactory method of solving this problem of decreasing taxes and increasing tax delinquent land. Some states are taking them over and creating state reserves—state forests and state parks. Counties and other political units are being urged to follow a similar course, but, because of the precarious financial situation in many states and communities, it is being urged with increasing support that the greater part of this land be taken over by the Federal Government and added to the National Forests. The so-called Copeland Report, representing the latest and most detailed study of the forest situation by the United States Forest Service, recommends additions to the National Forests that will more than double their area. But here, again, the obstacle lies in the old familiar field of finance, for such purchases will require staggering sums of money—or sums that would have been staggering before the advent of CWA, PWA, and other costly alphabetical combinations.

Depressions, like other forms of adversity, make strange bedfellows, and today the lumber industry, which was once so unalterably opposed to extensive ownership of forest lands by the Federal Government, is pleading with tears in its voice that this very step be taken. The reason, of course, is not far to seek—such purchases will lighten the industry's own burden of millions of acres of forest land, on which it is forced to pay taxes, and from which it derives little or no revenue. Regardless of the virtues of the plan or obstacles to it, the fact remains that, should it be carried out, a vast recreational area will be made available for development on sound and natural principles.

The other school of thought regarding recreational development proposes a drastic change in the fundamental principle of public ownership of wild life. This school maintains that the most satisfactory solution lies in obtaining legislation that will give to the private land owner full control over whatever wild life his land may contain. In this way it would be to the land owner's interest to protect his property from fire and other hazards, and to keep it well stocked with fish and

116

game, as a source of income from the sale or lease of fishing and hunting permits. In this way the financial burden would be shifted from government to the private individual. The person who sought to obtain hunting and fishing would have to pay for the privilege a sum commensurate with the cost of maintaining it.

There is much to be said for this point of view. It would place the burden of expense as a direct charge upon recreation itself, and would tend to destroy the old silly conception that public services cost nothing. The strength of this old conception has already been pointed out in connection with the proposal to build sewage disposal plants to be paid for by the users. The same example points to the strength of an inherent prejudice against paying as you go.

So much for both points of view. Probably the correct solution lies somewhere between the two. It is undoubtedly unfortunate that those who can least afford to pay for outdoor recreation live where there is most difficulty to extensive public development on a free basis. In our consideration of the wise use of the New Leisure it becomes increasingly evident that the correct solution of our wild life and conservation problem is of the utmost importance in our national economy. For we

117

can not make adequate progress towards supplying outdoor recreation for all without meeting the land problem face to face in its entirety, and dealing with it not as a mere furbelow of economic development, to be set aside until everything else is cleared up, but as one of the myriad pieces of the entire puzzle picture, in which no one piece is any more or less important than any other.

There are many who enjoy the outdoors, yet care neither to shoot nor to fish, and their numbers are increasing yearly. For these one of the outdoor interests or hobbies which is constantly gaining in popularity is photography. Hunting wild animals or birds with a camera instead of a gun offers a fascination that has a direct appeal to thousands. Many a sportsman who formerly concentrated on killing has taken up camera hunting as a more practical and advanced pursuit. Camera hunting of big game is indeed more advanced than shooting, because in many respects it is more difficult. To secure good photographs, even with lenses called telescopic or telephoto, the hunter must approach nearer to his quarry. He must contrive different ways and means of accomplishing this. He must give more consideration than ever to the laws of nature, and more careful study to the habits of his quarry. The compensations, to be sure, are proportionately greater. The man who hunts deer or bear with a gun probably shoots at his first opportunity. Thereupon, if he is a good shot, the hunt is over. But the man with a camera gets not only that first shot, but often many others, probably nearer at hand, more interesting, more illuminating, more worthy of preservation. And, while the wild animal approaches closer and closer to his hiding place, many things may happen. Before the hunter's eyes there may be enacted a hundred variations of the drama of nature, motivated by hunger, battle, love-making, or motherhood. And, while we have referred to wild animal photography as being in many ways more difficult, these difficulties are not such as to be insurmountable to anyone who wants to follow a photographic hobby.

Hunting with a camera is admirably suited to the New Leisure, because it is not generally subject to game laws. It may be pursued in closed seasons and in open seasons. It may be practiced in the far-off wilds or close at home, for nature photography is an ideal pursuit for the suburban home and the backyard. Songbirds thrive upon association with mankind, wherever they are given reasonable protection and encouragement, and their performances of love-making, home-making,

and in the rearing of their young offer a never-
ending pageant at our very doors. The knack of
photographing them is not difficult. The nature
photographer soon learns the tricks of a set camera operated at a distance by a string. He tames
his subjects with food and with nesting material,
and resorts to a variety of other interesting tricks
to make them more satisfactory models.

In the photography of small mammals there is
a wide and popular field in which the pioneering
photographer learns to construct live traps and
then photographs his subjects in homemade pens
or cages, arranged to appear as their natural sur-
roundings and without showing confining bars.
The photography of insects has been a hobby for
many, and, although for this branch of nature
photography and for several others, special equipment is required, surprisingly good results may be
obtained with no more investment than a good
gun or a set of fishing tackle would call for.

Photography of flowers opens up an equally
varied and alluring field. Lastly, there are those
phases of photography that are related to art—
the study of landscapes, of unusual lighting, and
many side lines. Nature photography is already
organized on the basis of clubs for creating the
spice of competition. It offers rewards in the form

of prizes and publication. Magazines and newspapers are constantly in the market for unusual photographs, and, while nature photography, as a general rule, is not among the best of professions for earning a livelihood, it does appear as an ideal leisure-time activity that holds the added advantage of a possible financial return.

The study of bird migrations through bird-banding is another popular nature hobby encouraged by the United States Government through the Bureau of the Biological Survey. Private individuals are permitted to become coöperators and are licensed to trap wild birds in non-injurious traps. The Government furnishes bands bearing numbers, one of which is put about a leg of each bird captured. The bird-bander gains satisfaction not only from noting the return of what might be called his own birds, but also from time to time is intrigued by capturing a bird bearing someone else's band, which bird may have come from a long distance away. Bird-banding includes not only songbirds, but also migratory birds and game birds of all species. It serves as a check upon numbers, food supplies, diseases and habits, and permits wise control from conservation and sporting points of view. Wild ducks and geese, gulls, and similar birds show migrations reported in this manner extending across the length of the continent and even into South America. Occasionally birds banded in America have been picked up in Europe. The thrill of being a party to such a find is a very real one. All band numbers are reported to Washington, and the Biological Survey informs each coöperator where any particular band originated. So interchange and migrations are recorded and made part of a vast scientific study of the habits of wild birds—a study of very considerable economic value to the country as a whole, because of the recognized importance of songbirds in the control of agricultural pests. And this economic value to the country as a whole makes bird-banding an ideal pursuit for those whose heritage still includes the puritanic inhibition against non-productive activities, for, since this occupation has a *practical* value, there need be none of the hesitation and misgivings that would otherwise beset some of us in pursuing a purely leisure outlet.

Bird-banding appeals to many older and comparatively inactive people, and furnishes them with an engaging substitute for actual hunting. Typical of this class is a woman living in a far valley of the Catskill Mountains, where each day she sits upon the porch with a dozen strings fastened to a ring close beside her. Each string leads out to a different part of the orchard or garden near at hand, where traps are located on the ground or in the trees. During the spring and fall migrations wild birds come into the traps every few minutes in search of food or water, and, as the traps become occupied, the woman unhooks the ring and the traps close. She goes out, bands her prizes, sets them free, returns to her chair and opens all her traps again. In this way she has been furnished with many hours of delightful and exciting occupation; and, at the same time, she is contributing her own mite to the sum total of knowledge in regard to bird movements.

Other nature interests include collecting, and, although the value of collecting, as a whole, is to be made the subject of a subsequent chapter, nature collecting itself offers a combination of the ordinary values of a collecting hobby, together with an actual pioneering participation in the out-of-doors. For it may be pursued in connection with camping, hiking, or mountain climbing, and the range of subjects to be collected is almost unlimited, extending throughout the gamut of ornithology, zoölogy, botany, mineralogy, anthropology, and many others.

Much of our knowledge of geological history

123

and of prehistoric peoples comes from amateur collecting that is later centralized through museums and institutions for research. Fragments of pottery and basket work, when pieced together with other relics of the past, reveal to us the ages of man. Gradually there is being evolved a definite chronology of early man in the western United States, based upon a study of the growth rings of trees. From thousands of specimens it has been possible to piece together a story of good years and years of drought in the Southwest, a story made visible today by the effect on the growth rings of trees. The overlapping of these sections with known events has gradually made it possible to check up on time as far back as the birth of Christ. Cross-sections of old roof poles found in human dwellings, when exhumed, fit into a definite chronicle of human events. Here is a field in which an outdoor hobby is of an immense scientific as well as recreational value.

The question of collecting as a nature hobby should not be passed over without a note of caution. For, while the collection of inanimate objects and of insects is not destructive and often highly creative, the indiscriminate collection of wild flowers, plants, mammals, and birds is contrary to the principles of conservation, and is inimical to the maintenance of outdoor recreation for the future. Unfortunately, the collecting instinct has done much toward the extermination of rare species, for the rarer the species, the more highly it is prized by collectors, and the greater the incentive to secure it. Such a situation leads rapidly toward complete extermination of a species, and in certain states, such as Florida, where unusual species of bird, mammal and plant life once abounded, collectors have offered such high prices for specimens that the state has found it necessary to step in and enact strict regulations. Unfortunately, even these restrictions have been too late. In like manner, it has been the common deplorable practice to encourage boys and girls to collect specimens of wild flowers, which, though constructive for the individual child, is undeniably destructive for all who may follow. Certain wild flowers that propagate in large quantities by seed can withstand a great deal of collecting, but others, which grow from the roots, are usually destroyed in the process of collecting, and are gradually disappearing. The loss of any species, however lowly, inevitably detracts from the potential value of our outdoor assets.

There are still other people who obtain their pleasure and satisfaction merely in being able to look after themselves in the out-of-doors, for it develops their self-sufficiency to conquer mountains and deserts as the pioneers did. They obtain from these activities the soul-comfort of contact with nature, and, at the same time, the satisfaction of bringing their bodies through difficult situations unscathed. But even in such forms of recreation the very presence of wild things, the sight of an animal or a leaping fish serves to dramatize the picture, creates an imperishable memory, and enriches the entire journey. So here, also, there is need for clear, uncontaminated streams where one may camp and drink without the disillusioning sight of an old shoe or a piece of sewage drifting by. There is need to maintain a balance of forests to prevent erosion and to provide welcome shade. There is need to uphold the vision of solitude, unmarred by rushing automobiles and the tawdry trappings of civilization.

For more than a decade now we have been warned that this mad age of speed and noise is breaking down the mental structure of the race. Sociologists and physicians point to rapidly increasing numbers of mental derangements, to our overflowing asylums and institutions. They call attention to the mounting cost of caring for the unfit. Should we compare this cost with the probable cost of making available preventive recreation, rest, and peace, we are confronted with the fact that billions spent now for institutions for the insane would be fully adequate to supply the necessary means of preventing most of the insanity.

Now, were this a small, densely populated country, it might be impossible to offer outdoor recreation in a natural environment for everyone. But America presents no such difficulty. There are acres of wild land for every man and woman in the country. There is abundant opportunity to provide recreational development and to restore the sanity, happiness, and contentment that outdoor recreation can bring.

Each year outdoor recreation gains wider recognition, and it may be that with the coming years we shall see this type of activity supplant the present "Big Four"—the automobile, the moving picture, the radio, and competitive sports organized on a grand, "go-getter" scale. But at present one is forced to confess that Americans spend two-thirds of their entire recreation budget on these four methods of leisure-time enjoyment.

Even outdoor recreation will require a degree of management and control. Like every other form of activity, it falls naturally and easily into facile and false channels. The very idea that the best way to promote popularity of hunting is to make killing easy has been proved unsound, but it is more or less typical of the popular development of the whole outdoor field. The abuse of modern transportation, particularly the automobile, is destructive not merely to the game, but also to the benefit sought by those who pursue it. We all admit the importance of physical development, for we promote it through gymnasiums and through various sports. Yet in hunting and fishing we banish all necessity for physical exertion by making killing easy and building highways directly to the game, and so place the emphasis upon the killing rather than upon the pleasure and thrill of the hunt. Naturally, when we make it possible for one man to return home and boast that he shot a hundred ducks on a single trip of two or three days' duration, or that he caught his limit of fish in an hour, or shot his deer within a hundred yards of his automobile, the statement tends to dim the far greater accomplishment of some other man who may have spent nights out under the stars, who was forced to learn the secret ways of the wild things, and who conquered a thousand natural obstacles before he finally made his kill.

It is human nature to judge superficially by re-
128

sults. It is human nature to demand conditions for oneself as easy as those enjoyed by another, for the urge to civilize is a pioneer instinct, even though the germ of destruction may lie therein. It is an urge which defeats the ends and benefits of pioneering itself.

Some there are who claim that it is necessary to make hunting and fishing easy because the average man cannot spare the time to enjoy it, except in the shortest, simplest way. But, if we follow that line of reasoning, why not eliminate original art in favor of snapshot photography, or creative music in favor of a phonograph? The contention that one lacks time for recreation is, in this new economic world of ours, an atavistic one. It is a throwback to an old belief, a reversion to a principle that has been outworn. What the Machine Age has changed it will continue to change. Man, confining his attention to production, can produce today more than his needs, even under the stimulation of highly developed advertising arts. True, this condition, with its attendant leisure, has not yet come for all, but it is on the way. The world has long been drifting toward a leisure class and a working class, the former obtaining more and more leisure, the latter standing still. It is a situation that will be no longer tolerated. Leisure must and will be shared. If it is shared on a basis of hours per day, it can and will be shared on a basis of working days, and working weeks, so that, when properly directed and organized, leisure may be concentrated in such a way as to render it suitable for the pursuit of those leisure activities that require more than a chance hour here and there. It is for this kind of leisure, as well as for vacant moments interspersed with the daily task, that our outdoor recreation must plan and must envisage, or else the New Leisure will have failed of obtaining for mankind its most abundant and lasting benefits.

VI

THE NEW LEISURE AND SPORTS

GAMES and sports have offered the most popular conception of recreation. From earliest times they have been godfathered by the most enthusiastic proponents of national defense and militarism. The physical ideals of ancient Greece and Rome laid enormous stress upon the maintenance of bodily health that for centuries proved so valuable an asset in times of war; but in America, until the time of the Civil War, calisthenics and gymnastics, carried on with the purpose of providing physical training and physical fitness, received the major part of the emphasis, and it was not until the middle eighties that outdoor sports attained national significance in this country.

Today, although the old background and militaristic attitudes are still prominent, the value of sports and games as an outlet for natural human energies is becoming increasingly stressed. More than ever this aspect of recreational activity merits increasing attention because of the change that has occurred in our modes of living and in our physical environment. America, once a nation of small rural homes with ample backyard and schoolyard playgrounds, has now centered its population in great cities. Natural playgrounds no longer exist where they are most needed, and the playground features of our recreational problem are becoming more and more artificial, requiring special financial investment and professional supervision.

Properly indulged, outdoor games cultivate health, but beyond this they serve a social function that is becoming of increasing importance as the complexities of our civilization multiply. For they develop concentration, persistence, good sportsmanship, and a social attitude considerate of human relationships. They are a type of play appealing to both young and old, and embody in the highest degree both a release of energy and the spice of competition. In this country we have built up an attitude toward sports which gives them an emphasis unequaled by any other forms of leisure activity. The number of pages devoted by our press to reporting sports events is the best evidence that our nation is not only sports-conscious, but almost super-sports-conscious. As a matter of fact, if there is a criticism to be made of outdoor sports

132

in America today, it would be to the effect that our primary fault lies in over-organizing and over-selling their competitive feature. Sport has been commercialized to the point where it is one of the greatest industries of the United States. It has been estimated that the annual expenditure for sporting and athletic goods alone amounts to over $500,000,000.

Sport has been professionalized not merely in regard to participation, but more particularly from the point of view of showmanship, so that the promotion aspect surpasses every other in seeming importance. Sport as a public spectacle is not new, for it dates back at least as far as the Olympics, and, as in the days of ancient Greece and Rome, we find that what originally began as a healthful recreation for enjoyment by the many has inevitably drifted into the amphitheater stage, has become a series of spectacles, a kind of glorification of battle, an appeal to elementary animal instincts. It is another instance of the fact we have already noted—man needs an antagonist in play as well as in work. This is true even in his vicarious participation in sport. For at baseball games the audience is expected to derive its interest from bitter partisanship, from the lust of witnessing a battle, and from the thrill of victory at any cost.

The temper of an audience at a boxing or professional wrestling match—both recently popular forms of exploiting gladiatorial battle—can hardly be called a creative one. To a certain extent it is recreational, in that it certainly tends to wipe out every thought of care and worry, and refreshes the mind of the observer, but its value is negative rather than positive.

Even in the case of college football, which, in spite of professional competition, still remains the most popular conception of that game, the ratio of participation to mere on-looking is not more than one to one thousand, and of each thousand on-lookers, only a very few are primarily interested in the sport for its true value—for its health-building, discipline, coördination, and its element of human relationships. The great overwhelming majority are there with the same frame of mind as those very similar audiences who cheered on the Roman gladiators and turned thumbs down on the conquered. We do not definitely demand blood today, but we want a score at almost any cost, and the motto of your average sports audience today no less than in the time of the Caesars still remains *vae victis*.

Now, should this picture seem at all a gloomy one, let us remember that it is only because we lose sight of the painfully slow process that goes to make up human development. Football rules, for example, are constantly being revised for greater safety, for the development of the game from a scientific viewpoint. The number of field judges, umpires, linemen is really an indication of the attempt to control this development along sane lines. Constant efforts are being made to put football and other games on a fairer, more sportsmanlike basis, with agreements to rule out the old atavistic gladiatorial policies. We find, also, a broadening of the basis for sports. Amateur track meets, hockey games, and many other contests are obtaining an increasing share of public interest, while the blood-lust complex is being confined to such distinctly elemental affairs as professional boxing and wrestling.

Yet, just as in the Olympics of ancient Greece and in the Roman gladiatorial combats, trouble still exists in the excess of promotion from the on-looking rather than from the participation standpoint. Nor does this contradict our previous admission that there is an undeniable recreational value in the psychological process of substitution which covers nearly all entertainment through the eye. We have to admit that for the physically and mentally weary this form of recreation is of great

135

benefit. But what we must see in organized sports is an example of the danger of too much publicity and over-stimulation of the competitive instinct. To be sure, pioneering and the pioneering instinct of our nation were primarily competitive, and perhaps organized sport has been forced to absorb more than its share of the competitive functions of this pioneering instinct. Competition with nature has been turned into competition with men and, until there are more opportunities for competition on a constructive basis, our excess competitive instinct is bound sooner or later to run riot.

Much of what purports to be an interest in sports is actually a manifestation of the gambling instinct—another pioneer trait. When gambling with life and death, and with the forces of nature, is either discouraged or ceases to be an important part of daily living, men tend to gamble with whatever else is the nearest substitute that promises a psychic equivalent. The extent of this gambling instinct has recently been emphasized by the widespread move to repeal anti-gambling laws, which were never obeyed in spirit and have largely served to increase gambling hazards, generally at the expense of all those who are not "insiders."

Perhaps the most extensive form of gambling in this country—where national lotteries are barred

—is based upon horse racing, and horse racing really is a perfectly legitimate sport, wherein men participate both physically and mentally no less than the horses they train and ride. Since gambling is an expression of the competitive instinct, it is found not merely in professionally organized sports of the spectacle type, but throughout almost every game man has invented. Gambling is the *sauce piquante* which may be added to almost anything or nothing. There are games invented solely for gambling's sake, in which the elements of human participation are reduced to the minimum. These run from purely mechanized contrivances, such as roulette, to certain card games wherein the human participation amounts to nothing more than the simplest mental process combined with an ability to bluff. Even in gambling there exist certain recreational values from the point of view of refreshment and change of thought—a psychological value; but, if we are to classify gambling itself as a sport, we must admit that its weakness lies more in abuse than in use, and our present consideration deals primarily with gambling as an evidence of the disproportionate emphasis upon on-looking as opposed to participation in outdoor sports.

Sport in the form of games suffers from the fact

that facilities are lacking for actual participation by many more persons than are present. The modern tendency toward concentration of population in large cities makes it comparatively easy to witness a spectacle, but very difficult for the individual to participate in a similar activity. The problem resolves itself into a playground problem, a housing problem, a land problem, and the wise advance planning and supervision of sports on a basis very different from that of promotion along present lines. For a solution of the difficulty we must turn back to the public schools, to the home itself.

The use of the New Leisure for participation in games offers a problem but little different from the use of the New Leisure in agriculture, in nature, or in any other of its numerous aspects. It requires a conception of objectives and a gradual evolution on the basis of study and planning. There is little virtue in criticizing the modern development of sports from the moral standpoint, when its greatest limitations are based upon inadequacy of physical means for improvement and extension.

An organization formerly called the Playground and·Recreation Association of America, and later reorganized as the National Recreation Association, has given much study to the play-

138

ground problem. This organization realized that playgrounds are as important for adults as for children, and that, in order for adults to appreciate and use them, they must be trained in games from childhood and made to realize that opportunity is available in this direction. Accordingly, the National Recreation Association, with its subsidiary organizations scattered throughout the land, has campaigned not only for school playgrounds, but also for playgrounds to be used by adults.

A survey of the leisure activities and desires of five thousand people located largely in eastern cities has been conducted by this National Recreation Association, and indicates very clearly the problem before us. Those answering the questionnaires stated not only what forms of leisure activities they were accustomed to enjoy, but also what they would like to do, if they could. Preëminent among the sports desired appeared tennis. Men and women expressed a wish to play—a wish largely unrealized because of the lack of available public tennis courts and the cost involved on a club basis. Tennis may require a smaller investment per participant than does golf, but the cash outlay is nevertheless beyond the means of thousands. Municipal tennis courts have been incorporated in the playground parks of many cities, but there is still need for far greater expansion.

Another sport emphasized in the same survey was swimming. It appeared seventh on the list of the total number reporting participation, nearly three thousand of the five thousand total giving it mention. But less than half this number reported frequent participation, although opportunities for swimming were desired by almost as many persons as tennis, and these two sports topped the desired list. Swimming, of course, appeals both to men and women, but under conditions of urban development it requires special facilities. The problem of supplying pools is fully comparable with that of furnishing other play facilities, and, although today there are more than 8,000 public and private pools in the United States, the opportunities for swimming still lag far behind the demand.

Our national game, of course, is baseball. An annual attendance of at least 20,000,000 at professional games places it in the first rank of American sports. As such, it has been commercialized to a greater degree than any other sport. Yet it has served a constructive purpose. Baseball has provided young America with idols—some, it is true, with feet of very common clay—and has inspired the youth of this country to play a game calling for team-play, skill, and sportsmanship. These qualities, inherent in the game of baseball, have made it endure, and for these qualities alone it should be fostered. In many cities this is being done through the promotion of amateur baseball leagues. For several years now the American Legion has promoted such leagues among the youngsters as part of its Americanism program. Many newspapers have sponsored leagues, with an eye to the circulation department, to be sure, but nevertheless with a fundamental recognition of the national affection we all have for the sport. Baseball with a soft ball and toothpick bat has recently been given impetus, even to the point of forming amateur leagues, and, since this variation of the national pastime requires less space for playing, it promises to attain ready popularity.

So baseball is a game worthy of primary consideration in any program of recreational character that has to do with the use of leisure. For the most part, its participants will be boys and men up to the age of forty, but the attendance at games by those whose age forbids them to play is in no sense a waste of leisure. The furtherance of any clean competitive sport is a contribution to the fundamental soundness of our citizenry.

141

The development of golf has created an outdoor sport which emphasizes the limitations of physical equipment, particularly the need for available space. It is curious that this game which, above all others, requires the largest area of playground per individual participant, has taken such thorough hold upon the American consciousness. Perhaps it represents our national tendency toward extremes.

Of course, golf has always possessed an important virtue in being a game not too strenuous or athletic for people who have become largely sedentary. During the times of prosperity it promised to attain an almost unbelievable growth. Private capital seemed to be available in unlimited quantities, and municipal financing was apparently thriving in uncontrolled expansion. So private golf courses and public golf courses were easily acquired, and dotted the face of the whole countryside. With the depression golf received a setback at the very time when it might have performed its greatest service in distracting human minds from economic troubles. Golf, as exemplified by private club membership, with all its social implications and demands, was too expensive to be made available to everyone. At any rate, relative values were so suddenly and abruptly upset that the cold necessity of panic rather than fair judgment tended to change the whole map of public participation in this sport. Whatever is the true value of golf and its suitability for the different ages of man should maintain it as an outdoor sport suitable for the New Leisure; and, whatever the rapid rise of golf has done, it has at least proved that it is possible to secure playgrounds for adults. It has established that general participation in outdoor sports is an attainable goal.

With the recent development of interest in outdoor life has come a new appreciation of the value of the nation's waterways for recreation. Beginning with the days of early settlers, our waterways were regarded as nothing more than aids to transportation, with the result that our city waterfronts have been largely turned over to commercial and industrial use. Little or no attention was given to developing waterways and beaches for recreation purposes, and long before city planning was adopted, our larger centers had become the least attractive portions of urban development. Waterfronts were lined with docks, warehouses, and wharves, hideous to behold and of commercial value only. The only recreational use they saw was alcoholic.

With later years, vigorous protests have arisen

143

against this exploitation of waterfronts by private interest to the exclusion of their use for recreation purposes. Progress is already being made toward developing attractive parks and beaches in these very localities. Chicago offers such an example, where new land has been made for miles along Lake Michigan's shore. Yet, notwithstanding present progress, this country lags woefully behind European nations in appreciation and use of waterfronts for recreational purposes.

The growth of bathing beaches has been accompanied by a similar increase in the use of watercraft for pleasure purposes. Yacht clubs now number over four hundred and fifty, many of them maintaining splendid club houses, providing harbors for various kinds of watercraft, from small sailing vessels to palatial motor yachts.

Among competitive sports that have found varied favor in different parts of the country and possess excellent possibilities for the use of leisure time are soccer, lacrosse and cricket. Ice hockey should be given greater attention than it is outside of college and professional ranks in sections where climate permits a sufficiently extended season. As a matter of fact, outdoor winter sports dependent upon snow and ice are limited to the northern states and have made greatest headway where low temperatures are fairly continuous throughout the winter months. Our modern playground movement, having its origin in large northern cities, was at first concerned with summer rather than winter sports, and outdoor winter sports were left wholly to the initiative of the individual. The striking change that has occurred in outdoor winter sports during the past twenty years is the result of organized public effort to provide adequate facilities.

Bicycle racing has waned in popularity, but bicycle riding itself has recently enjoyed a renaissance in various parts of the country, and promises to provide a part in providing healthful use of leisure time.

There are a number of more or less highly organized outdoor sports that partake partly of the nature of sport, yet which fall partly into the category of outdoor or nature interests. Among these are motor-boating, sailing, horseback riding —sports that may be pursued with or without the competitive feature, so that they become either games or hobbies, as the participant wills. The presence of potential competitive aspects is desirable, but, at the same time, the non-competitive recreational features are deserving of study and attention because of the very fact that in other fields competition has been over-emphasized. In

145

motor-boating and sailing we may note a further overlapping of recreational values in that they usually are related to mechanical hobbies of a constructive nature, for these sports may involve boat building, aerodynamics, and engineering as closely related amateur leisure-time hobbies.

Perhaps the healthiest sign in the very recent development of athletic sport is the growing popularity of the games that appeal more to the participants than to the observers. Another trend of national significance is the growing interest in outdoor sports of a less strenuous type that are suitable for mature people of both sexes and for those unable to indulge in violent exercise.

Indoor games, naturally, lack many of the direct health-building characteristics of outdoor sports, but their importance is not to be overlooked. For, aside from their social value in human relationships, they possess most of the qualifications that we have set up for governing a wise use of the New Leisure. True, the energy that they consume is chiefly mental rather than physical, but they add much pleasure and zest to living, supply an outlet for expression of mental superiority in a manner that seldom injures the rights of others or imperils their security of livelihood. Bridge, as a game, has become one of the great national pastimes, carrying in its wake a demand for professional teachers, and including as much form and paraphernalia as may be claimed by many outdoor sports. Card games, in general, of course, are among the oldest forms of play known to mankind, and, as such, are respected and acclaimed by the public everywhere, until the annual expenditure for decks of cards has reached the staggering total of $20,000,000. The very antiquity of cards as an indoor game has gradually built up an association with the gambling instinct already mentioned, so that many, in estimating recreational value, are prone to discount it and to oppose all forms of recreation that happen to be attended by a recognized opportunity for gambling. This is unfortunate, because unnecessary.

Indoor games seem to be even more susceptible to faddism than outdoor games. The recent craze for ping-pong, or table tennis, is a case in point. This single game rose in a few months from a comparatively obscure form of parlor entertainment to a national enterprise, with local, state, and national tournaments, silver cups, press notices, and all the high pressure trappings. It may be that the faddist characteristics of ping-pong, like certain faddist characteristics of golf, are really based upon a primary adaptability to human needs. For

147

there have been few indoor games better suited to the fullest development of recreational values than ping-pong. It is an exception among indoor games, in that it possesses a physical development value as well—a value that can hardly be escaped unless the participants employ someone to pick up the balls for them.

Bowling is an indoor sport of immense popularity, which provides good exercise, but, unfortunately, is rather expensive and usually practiced in smoke-filled alleys that more or less destroy the physical benefits. Basketball and handball are both indoor sports of considerable merit, although the extension of basketball is hindered because of the physical facilities required for it.

We have discussed the various types of indoor and outdoor play in some detail, because the New Leisure will have to face the problem of sports and games of all kinds. A wise direction, an honest attempt to organize them for a more extensive public participation will include a wide variety. It will recognize that playgrounds and recreational centers for both children and adults are essential and not merely the phenomena of artificial prosperity. If there is a public duty to provide security of livelihood for each individual in accordance with an idealistic interpretation of Constitutional rights, it would seem a positive necessity to interpret the same hypothesis on the broader grounds that guarantee not merely the right of security, but also a reasonable equality of opportunity towards fuller living. An opportunity to participate in sports and games is, perhaps, as much the right of every individual as any other right he may claim to possess, for, whether such participation is or is not a moral right, the fact remains that for the welfare of the state—a welfare bound up in a reasonable contentment of its people—the nation must recognize the need to play. Play is the balance wheel of every economic system. It is the governor that keeps the machine of economics from racing uncontrollably on to its own destruction.

VII

EVALUATING A HOBBY

An INSURANCE expert, one of the high officials of the National Surety, Company, speaking to a group of business men, made the statement that the man with a hobby is considered an unusually good risk. This, he pointed out, was true not merely from the standpoint of health, but also from the moral standpoint. The National Surety Company issues bonds to guarantee performance of contract, to protect banks against peculation or theft by employees, and to insure corporations in general against the possible dishonesty of their own treasurers. This speaker explained that the statistics of his company proved that a man with an outside interest or hobby was less likely to get into trouble than a man without one. The company attributed this to the fact that the hobbyist is too busy with his own pet subject to be concerned about taking other people's money. This, of course, is a hardboiled and practical viewpoint, which tells rather less than half the story, but it does point to one of the salient potentialities of the New Leisure.

Much economic difficulty, much dishonesty and criminality finds its origin in an unbalanced life. We know that lack of opportunity along legitimate lines often causes men, women and children to become anti-social and criminal. Often the lack of opportunity is economic—it is an inability to earn a livelihood or to maintain a desired standard of living—but this purely physical interpretation leaves unexplained a great deal of everyday dishonesty, as well as many of our greatest crimes. In these cases the reason seems to lie not so much in the lack of economic opportunity as in the urge for some outstanding accomplishment and in a desire for recognition and fame, however humble. It is a perversion of the natural restlessness of human beings. We pass it off by saying that criminals are usually deranged mentally—which, as far as it goes, is the truth; but we also refer to persons with some strange hobby as "nuts," when, as a matter of fact, that hobby is chiefly a means of working off restlessness or "steam" in a constructive manner unharmful to society and actually creative for the individual himself.

Although we have maintained that the attitude

151

of Americans toward leisure as a health-builder has been created and upheld largely as an aid to production and business success, we can not fail to recognize health as an essential factor to the attainment of happiness and contentment. Neither can we disregard the implications of health from a moral standpoint, from the point of view of a constructively social value, as opposed to the anti-social, criminal influence of ill health. So it is a mistake to regard outdoor recreation and physical exercise as activities that serve only as means to the attainment of muscles and school-girl complexions. The greatest experts of medicine and surgery now recognize that the psychological factor is of at least equal importance. Proofs of this are increasing daily. Remarkable cures have been worked out by introducing a patient to some hobby or interest that will take his mind from himself, from his troubles, his worries, and direct it into constructive channels. As a matter of fact, the dictionary's definition of "hobby" as "something in which one takes an extravagant interest" gives us the key to many kinds of strange and almost miraculous recoveries and cures that have been brought about by introducing patients to interests more stimulating than their own pulse and temperature.

Recently at the Elmira Reformatory in New

York State a number of cases of hip disease and infantile paralysis were greatly aided by introducing hobbies among the boys. Six boys were chosen from among those in various stages of these diseases, and, in addition, a boy who was considered incurable. The particular hobby introduced was postage stamp collecting. The six boys showed marked improvement from the first, and all were finally discharged, fully cured, six months before boys similarly afflicted who did not collect. The one whose case had been considered hopeless made marked improvement.

So a facile attitude of superior condescension toward hobbies is not enough, and it behooves us to give serious consideration to every kind of hobby as a possible constructive use of the New Leisure, no matter how foolish any of them may appear to those of us who think we do not care to ride them. Men great and small have pursued a long and varied list of strange leisure activities. Some run to research in local family genealogies. Some collect door knockers, bird cages, fans, pewter porringers, colored glass, and hooked rugs. The gamut of collecting hobbies runs from samplers to match-box lids, from empty liquor bottles to old masters. Some, on the other hand, find their greatest pleasure in the actual creation of physical

153

things with their hands—from radios to ship-models, rabbit hutches to etchings. Often, to the hard-headed, practical man of affairs, the "nut" with a hobby may appear a freak or an eccentric, but in the deeper analysis every hobbyist has in his makeup something of the true scientist. Turn him around and look him over for what he really is. He is giving up his time to research, to the pursuit of knowledge, and to widening the horizons of his own particular field.

Hobbies may be said to fall into three more or less overlapping fields. One is the acquiring of knowledge, which is, after all, the collection and integration of facts. Another is the collecting of objects, and still another is the creating of things. Any one of these three types can satisfy man's desire for power. Whether he achieves that desire by seeking to learn all there is to know about the universe, or merely to know more than anyone else about the fauna of his immediate neighborhood, whether he builds a cathedral or a dog-kennel, whether he collects modern match covers or ancient Egyptian pottery, he is exerting his intellect, and each addition to his hobby brings him that ever-satisfying sense of accomplishment.

Acquiring knowledge as a hobby led Newton to discover the law of gravity, and Darwin the origin of the species, but in its deepest sense the pursuit of knowledge is too austere a hobby to be of much interest to plain John Doe. His mind has not been trained for it.

Neither, for many, is the actual creation of things with the hands a satisfactory leisure-time pursuit, for, though the urge to create is one of the earliest impulses found in children, not many of us ever acquire sufficient manual deftness to obtain any gratification from this type of creative endeavor.

But, though neither of these two classes of hobbies in themselves appeal to the average man, collecting, which is a combination of the two—the acquiring of knowledge in a definite field and the creation of a tangible entity—is and always has been one of the most widely followed of hobbies. It is one of the earliest known, and can be said to be almost instinctive. It has been handed down through the ages from the prehistoric man who collected sea shells and pebbles to the man of enormous wealth, who today collects a great library of rare and priceless books.

In addition to bringing the collector the feeling of power that results from increased knowledge and from actual creation, collecting hobbies introduce the spice of competition. For almost every

strange collecting idea there are many counter-
parts, and collectors drift together into clubs to
exchange material, hold meetings, elect officers,
award medals to each other, and publish newspapers and magazines devoted to their own particular interests. Many of the greatest leaders of our
nation and throughout the world have been hobby-
ists of some sort. They have made truly great collections of all sorts of things, from preserved
butterflies to paintings. One of the best known collectors in the world is King George of England,
who in his youthful days began to collect postage
stamps. During the World War he decided to give
this up as a luxury which he could forego, in view
of the sacrifices that everyone was then making.
But, as the war went on, the King began to brood
over its horror and found himself unable to sleep.
At the advice of medical attendants, he once again
turned to his collection and found in it the only
thing that could afford him peace of mind and respite from sleeplessness. Another well-known collector who found his hobby of great psychological
value as a rest from care was Theodore Roosevelt.

The democracy of collecting has always been
one of the truest democracies in the world—the
wealthiest man meets the poorest to discuss inves-
tigations and objects of interest and value along

156

their own particular line. They meet on common ground; they talk a language of their own; perhaps they trade, but they do so with mutual respect. It is estimated that in the United States alone there are several million collectors of postage stamps. Because we hear of the immense monetary value of various collections made by the great of the world, it is not to be supposed that collecting is a hobby for the rich only. Of course, from the viewpoint of a few outstanding experts, millions of collectors may be tyros, but nevertheless they subscribe to publications devoted to their particular hobby, they trade and interchange and hold exhibits. They obtain for their efforts quite as much satisfaction as do the very famous few. For collecting of any sort is a game in which the advantage lies largely in diligence of search, persistence, and luck. Money alone will not supply the lack of these. The mere ownership of a collection is nothing except possibly a financial asset and in itself gives little pleasure or satisfaction. Even the museum value is small, as compared with the pleasure that came from the making and the doing. To be sure, certain kinds of collecting lie within the grasp of the rich alone, because the few objects collected have high cash value. Some rich collectors actually perform their work by proxy and employ agents to do the real work for them. This, of course, is not the sort of collecting that we refer to as democratic, yet it can not be denied that to the extent the rich collector gives thought and constructive attention to his hobby he directs his energy into channels unharmful to society and at the same time of benefit to himself.

Perhaps the most widespread collecting hobby in the world is that of collecting postage stamps, a hobby referred to by the collectors themselves as philately. So generally pursued is it that "philately" and "hobby" have become almost synonymous terms. And, while there is scarcely any other hobby less appealing to an outsider, it is more capable of arousing ardent interest in its followers than any form of collecting. Considered narrowly, nothing would seem more commonplace than stamps. The postman brings them every morning, and, when the mail is opened, they meet a swift, inglorious end in the wastebasket. Thought of superficially, it seems ridiculous that anyone should want to collect them; but for the inquiring and studious mind postage stamps develop a host of fascinating complications and alluring potentialities. Beginning with youth, the girl or boy who takes up stamp collecting is confronted with a practical application of geography far more fascinating than any school book could ever be. He learns the names of countries and finds out where they are. Subconsciously and quite painlessly a knowledge of history enters in—the history of the whole world since postage stamps began less than a century ago, and subjects commemorative of important historical events are among the most important for pictorial representations on postage stamps. There are the old states that made up the German Empire before Frederick the Great, nearly all of which once had their own postage stamps. There is the history of every war of modern times, of revolutions and of the Great War itself. What of German colonies that are no longer German? You will find the whole story written first in the printing over or "surcharging" of old stamps to show new political control, and finally in the appearance of entirely new issues. What became of little Servia, where the Great War started? It is all there on the stamps. Of course, no one collects postage stamps simply as a means of learning geography, history, and political economy. The point is that interests derived from other phases of this hobby are much increased when it is realized that the stamp collector has become familiar with people, places, and events ordinarily unknown to the non-collector.

It may be the color and beauty of stamps that first attract beginners. Perhaps part of the charm exists in the fact that stamps are a miniature portrait gallery of the famous men of the world. For one may find on postage stamps portraits ranging from King Darius on his throne to the newest president of the newest republic. Still another charm may lie in the realm of natural history, and, as a matter of fact, a book was once written on this single subject by James H. Lyons. With a painstakingness at which one marvels he found postage stamp pictures of stags, antelope, pheasants, monkeys, crocodiles, tapirs, rhinoceroses, hippopotamuses, vultures, lizards, and even snakes. There were camel stamps and caribou stamps, codfish stamps, seal stamps, and a host of others. Heraldry on stamps has been another fascinating subject, and, in the domain of more modern themes, we find that here, too, stamps play an illustrative part, for we have NRA stamps and dozens of commemorative issues for great exhibitions and anniversaries. One may collect religious stamps, sports stamps and agricultural stamps in infinite variety. As an offshoot, postage stamp collecting need not include only the stamps themselves, but the covers which bore them, and the postmark. When Lindbergh first flew the transcontinental mail after his Atlantic flight, the fact was advertised, and thousands of collectors sent letters for that particular delivery, in order that they might get them back from friends and keep them as souvenirs. Modern governments usually issue special postmarks or cancellations for such famous events as the earliest zeppelin flights, North Pole and South Pole expeditions, and many others. So in this way stamp collecting is coming to embody some of the charm of collecting autographs, which is another very widespread and popular hobby.

Because of the varied appeal of postage stamp collecting, it may be illustrative to consider it further as a typical example of a constructive hobby. Now, generally, collecting is an orderly procedure, requiring and cultivating neatness, accuracy, and attention to details, although its main charm for the collector probably lies in the lure of the chase, the detective instinct, the fascination of the hunt. Since the Stone Age, when some skin-clad ancestor of the race treasured in his cave more flint implements than he had actual use for, nearly everyone has been a collector. This is the root instinct of nearly all collecting. The collector needs a certain specimen to complete some specific group, and he hunts for it far and wide, communicating with other collectors the world over, in the hope that they may have a duplicate or at least be willing to trade. So the enthusiastic collector may hunt for years for a single object and then find it in the most unexpected place. Some extremely rare Hawaiian stamps were once found on letters that had been pasted up as wall paper to stop cracks in an old out-building.

Rarity alone is not always the sole charm, for association brings its own added allure. During our Civil War, for example, the Government, eager to raise money in every possible way, imposed a tax on patent medicines and then licensed the producing companies to print their own revenue stamps for the bottles or containers. The practice was in effect for a short time only, so that the stamps have become very rare; but even to this day they may be found on bottles stored away in some forgotten attic.

Advanced stamp collectors usually come to specialize on certain types of stamps of certain countries. By research they may endeavor to reconstruct the original condition of a sheet of stamps. This is not possible in the case of most modern stamps, but, in the early days of postage stamp making, the plate from which they were engraved was finished by hand, so that each one varied a little from its neighbor. By collecting blocks of stamps, in twos or threes or more, it is possible to determine which stamp was Number 6 from the right-hand upper corner, and to place it in its proper and original order. One American very well known for his public works dedicated an entire volume to a stamp of a single denomination of a certain country. He found that the original plate from which the stamps were printed had at some time been dropped or injured and later repaired by borrowing a part from still another plate. So he worked out the full history to the last and utmost detail—a story requiring the collection of thousands of specimens of that one individual stamp; but it brought him relaxation from his business and public service, and served to maintain his health during a time when it might otherwise have gone to pieces from worry and overwork.

This same collector, like many others, became expert in the methods of paper manufacture, for a stamp of a single denomination, reprinted over the years, is often printed on several different kinds of paper of various physical and chemical structure. So he learned the main principles of engraving and printing, in order to distinguish the samples which came to his attention. One day, shortly after the repeal of prohibition, he was offered a bottle of what was reputed to be good whiskey, bearing the United States revenue stamp. He looked at the bottle and said, "This is not good whiskey. It is not what it is represented to be."

"How do you know that?" asked the seller.

The answer was very simple. A glance at the United States revenue stamp on the stopper showed beyond doubt that the engraving or printing was of a type never turned out by the United States Government in the manufacture of revenue stamps, and, in addition, the paper was of the wrong kind. It could only mean that the stamp was a counterfeit; that the whiskey must be illegal and illegitimate.

The non-collector may view this story with amusement and ask, "What's the practical value of all this, aside from a possible ability to avoid poor whiskey?" Well, hobbyism is not supposed to possess a practical value. Its purpose is higher than that. It gives satisfaction to the hobbyist and to his associates, it brings them a sense of accomplishment, it wins them honor among those who appreciate their field, it brings them happiness, contentment, and a sense of creation.

Of course, collecting, like nearly every other occupation, has its financial side. Rare stamps and other rare objects have a definite market value listed in catalogues of dealers. Everyone recognizes that diamonds and other precious stones always have had a distinct investment value. In the case of diamonds, recent new discoveries have tended to depreciate the value of all diamonds in circulation, and the great South African Diamond Trust is forced to keep millions of dollars' worth locked up in its vaults to prevent their coming on the market and ruining the business. Postage stamps possess similar value, but, because they are not mined, the likelihood of new discoveries is extremely small; so they maintain their value without the creation of a trust for artificial stimulation.

It has been estimated that the greatest half dozen stamp collections in the United States possess an estimated value of from one million to two million dollars each. This value has not represented any such investment to the collectors themselves, although wealthy men have often spent a great deal on their hobbies. They have also contributed much in the way of time and brains, and this value has not been lost. The record price paid for any stamp is $32,500 paid for a British Guiana stamp of 1856. This has been called the rarest stamp in existence, but its

165

original value was exactly one cent. Some years ago, the Baron de Ferrari, an Austrian nobleman, died, bequeathing his stamps to the Berlin Museum. The French Government, realizing their value, seized the collection, sold it at auction, and raised one million, two hundred thousand dollars to be applied to the proceeds of reparations.

The fact is, stamp collecting, being one of the most popular and widespread of hobbies, has an actual financial side from the standpoint of money-making for the collector. In several countries there are a number of professional stamp dealers who make postage stamp collecting and postage stamp selling their means of livelihood, and nearly every collector gets some satisfaction from the financial potentialities of his activities. Thousands have made pocket money from their collections, yet they are the first to deny that they collect for any financial reason. The joy of collecting lies in the doing, and, for that reason, it is an ideal occupation for the New Leisure.

There are many other hobbies similar to philately. For, just as the collector of stamps may specialize in that commodity—in stamps of a certain country or period—so others of different tastes may collect prints, choosing individual fields, such as woodcuts, lithographs, etchings, dry-points, or some other technique, or may, provided they can afford it, concentrate on the work of some particular artist, such as Whistler or Pennell. Books, too, may be collected from various points of view.

Collecting of this sort, however, although it is not restricted solely to the rich, can not be called an ideal hobby for one who has a minimum amount of money to spend in collecting. And the best opportunity for collecting, where only time and effort need be spent, lies in the great world of the out-of-doors. In many parts of the country Indian arrowheads can be found. In others, strange and interesting geologic specimens, or ornithological or botanical prizes may be gained. There is hardly a phase of outdoor life that does not present an opportunity for a constructive hobby of this sort—opportunities to meet every taste and to suit every pocketbook.

We cannot pass the subject of collecting as a constructive force in the New Leisure without considering the subject of museums as a stimulation to individual endeavor and as an educational and entertainment medium. Generally, museums represent public participation in the encouragement of hobbies. They are the part that may be played by government and society, as a whole, in encouraging many uses of the New Leisure. There are historical museums, museums of art, museums of natural history, museums of engineering, museums of many other sorts, all of them having a part to play, not merely for the entertainment of the curious eye or for the harmless passing of leisure time, but also as educational centers that stimulate the will and provide the inspiration to collect and to build. The great American Museum of Natural History in New York is an enterprise supported partly by public and partly by private funds, that fulfills a host of functions. To its wealthy contributors it extends an opportunity to participate in research and exploration. To the rank and file of the city it extends an educational service of the highest order—a service confined not to the museum alone, but extended by traveling exhibits in city schools, by lectures and classes. The National Museum, the Field Museum of Natural History in Chicago, the Buffalo Museum, and many others throughout the country are performing the same sort of service in degrees that vary with their financial ability. Historical and art museums practice similar educational maneuvers in lending collections and giving instruction in appreciation. The Franklin Institute, in Philadelphia, has been building up a vast scientific museum where aid is offered to scientific hobbies of all sorts. It promotes model-building of airplanes and boats, holds meetings of clubs, and acts as an agent not only for the supervision of individual construction effort, but provides centers for the distribution of model-making materials.

The museums of the nation are the logical centers for collectors of all sorts, and it is through them that we may focus attention upon the constructive value of hobbies as a New Leisure force, and thus obtain the natural growth that would seem so desirable.

It is part of the very essence of leisure that one may not dictate its use, for, where dictation enters, personal initiative vanishes. And, recalling the simple definition that "Work is what one has to do, and play what one wants to do," it becomes evident that a stimulation of New Leisure activities must be indirect. It must not in any way appear forced upon the individual, else it would be no true leisure at all, but just because dictation and force represent faulty technique, it does not follow that New Leisure should be left to drifting and chance. True, we can not regiment it as an army is regimented. We can not reduce it to the narrow confines of militaristic or autocratic methods, but there is no ban against planning and preparation. There should be no objection to pa-

169

ternalistic financing of recreational stimuli and recreational means, for it has good precedence. For decades private wealth has endowed many museums, public libraries, and educational institutions, but dependence upon private endowment has never supplied the fundamentals of culture for all. The nation that plans for a New Leisure must consider whether the value of that leisure to the nation as a whole does not justify the use of public funds more extensively than ever dreamed of in the past.

VIII

THE NEW LEISURE AND ART, MUSIC, AND LITERATURE

It has been said that the essence of all national character is displayed through the art, music, and literature that it produces.

A young nation, peopled by pioneers, has little time for esthetic consideration. A growing commercial nation is a builder, erecting its monuments for posterity in terms of concrete and steel. So it is natural that Europeans should come to regard the skyline of New York City, superficially, at least, as the expression of our national spirit and character. They assume, quite correctly, that in the course of our commercial development we have groped our way to a unique conformity of art with our own intensely practical purposes. Certainly we have built great temples to the supposed fundamentals of life, as we have made life, and while adapting ourselves to our own conception of necessity, we have achieved an artistic ex-

171

pression different from that of any nation in the world—one that in its highest expression may be considered typically American. It is not that America has failed to produce other magnificent examples of art; it has both music and a literature that the rest of the world is learning to respect, but the fact remains that our most outstanding contribution has been in the realm of commercial architecture.

There are, of course, many who predict the end of our primarily industrial era. They tell us that the skyscraper must give way to the decentralization of population, to improvements in transportation, and, eventually, to the new principles of living which the New Leisure will engender. Our national youth, our pioneer period, and our age of expanding adolescence have all passed. We are approaching some kind of stabilization—not as a sudden transition, but rather a gradual evolution which nevertheless moves rapidly enough for us to see the high-lights and shadows of its unfolding development. There is no one to draw a hard black line between one period and another. There is no one to say that this or that was true, but is no longer so. Yet, subconsciously, we sense a difference, and the spectacle confronting us with the advent of the New Leisure enhances this sense of change. We may well consider its effect and profitably ponder the diverse forms into which these changes may be translated.

The day may be far distant before the skyline of New York ceases to typify the ultimate expression of the American spirit, but, little by little, another expression is evolving to take its place. Gradually, as a nation, we are becoming conscious of a growing spirit of revolt—a revolt we often hasten to suppress out of a spirit of loyalty to the practical ideas of the past; but we find ourselves increasingly conscious of beauty and increasingly annoyed when commercial exploitation destroys it. Unwilling to sacrifice our primary adherence to progress and to profit, we, as individuals, nevertheless begin to look with increasing favor upon the growth of numerous associations, leagues, and societies whose purpose is to promote the esthetic sense in many diverse fields. Thus it is not merely from the practical standpoint of most efficiently satisfying physical needs that city planning is being urged, but equally to achieve consistency, symmetry, and visual satisfaction. Commerce and industry, which, in the fast fading era of rugged individualism, were free to exploit nature and beauty purely for the achievement of transient and selfish aims, are now being criticized and reg-

173

ulated. Many of our states have passed zoning laws with this very end in view. True, the restrictions imposed have generally been inadequate and are little more than a framework upon which the future may build, but this framework has, at least, enabled a few progressive local communities to make tangible progress toward that very end.

One of the best examples is the commission in Westchester County, New York, which created the great parkways that lead to and from the city. Here is a wise and effective use of natural landscape, supplemented by artificial planting, and with sufficient land controlled on either side of the right of way to prevent commercial despoliation. The Cleveland super-park system represents a similar trend, and, on the Pacific Coast, the great Columbia Highway.

Examples of our growing esthetic consciousness are legion. We find a National Roadside Protection Committee (formerly the National Council for Protection of Roadside Beauty), with affiliated organizations in eleven states, all actively working to protect our highways from abuse by outdoor advertising, by the ubiquitous atrocity known as the hot-dog stand, by filling stations, dump-yards, and other olfactory and visual outrages. We find the United States Government,

174

through its Bureau of Public Roads, actually allocating part of its Federal Aid funds for planting and beautification of the highways which these funds have helped construct. We find publications actively devoted to urging esthetic considerations and creating powerful influence in favor of better zoning and more complete public control over private abuses. Numerous other individuals and organizations are helping to crystallize public opinion by urging persons who have the protection of beauty at heart to give preference in their buying to those commercial firms that have refrained from violating esthetic principles.

Now, the important thing is that almost none of this work of stimulating appreciation of beauty is fundamentally commercial. It is chiefly a result of New Leisure activity—devoted to public welfare, if you will, but more particularly to a championship of those indefinable, intangible values that are a national approach to true esthetic appreciation. Actually, the same New Leisure that gave us our first opportunity to cease "go-getting" long enough to see the ugliness that results from our rapid and wasteful economic development is bringing with it that modicum of free time so essential to any national consciousness of art. For art, in its broadest sense, is not confined to draw-

175

ing and painting and sculpture—these are only individual expressions that may accompany a general and often quite inarticulate consciousness of beauty.

The instinctive urge to create artistically is as old as man himself. Even before the Neolithic Age, the early Grimaldi and Cro-Magnon peoples expressed their own artistic gropings by drawings of mammoths and horses, and by little ivory and soapstone statuettes. Kings and queens of ancient Egypt patronized the arts and employed the highest talent they could find to decorate their temples and tombs. Art from the very first was a product of leisure; and, with the advent of the New Leisure, we find rapidly increasing numbers of those whose creative instincts seek outlet in drawing, painting, architecture, modeling, and design. Within the last few years the increasing sales of painting and drawing and modeling materials are an indication that the New Leisure has already met a widespread desire for artistic creation and the plastic arts. Even the dearth of education in art provided by our schools fails to prevent thousands suddenly presented with the gift of leisure from going forth with paper or canvas and brushes to essay their own interpretations of what art and beauty may be.

176

ART, MUSIC, AND LITERATURE

Opinions change rapidly in this changeable world of ours. While once we believed that no one could be an artist without a mane of flowing hair and a shirt-front decorated by a flamboyant tie; while once we felt that art was an expression of rare genius, with which no ordinary mortal might even hope to meddle, thousands are now discovering that it is not necessary to be a Rubens or a Rembrandt, in order to obtain enjoyment and satisfaction from artistic creation. The tide has set in strongly toward a true democratization of art, and with it we have emerged from our national inferiority complex, our slavish following of European models, and are beginning to turn to our own national life and environment for the subjects of artistic choice. And, since the love of things engenders a desire to reproduce them, many have found that drawing and painting are closely associated with the expression of numberless other interests. Thus, an interest in nature is expressed by amateurs not only in an attempt to paint landscapes, but also to recreate the individual flower one finds in gardens or fields. Their objective may be solely to retain a little of the fragile and fast-waning beauty of a blossom, or to record it for botanical purposes, but, whatever the purpose, the effect is the same—the urge toward artistic creation has been satisfied. There is also the human interest, concentrated in the study of human beings, human character, and many with the leisure time to express themselves turn naturally to attempts at portraiture, seeking the thrill that comes from the accurate portrayal with brush, or pencil, or clay, of a mental force or spiritual trait which seems to them significant. Even the instinct that turns more soberly to scientific interests finds its own expression in the wide and very useful realm of scientific art.

Indeed art is a hobby adapted to the chief interest of the performer, and, like all hobbies, finds its expression in many ways that at first seem passing strange. One finds men who specialize— not because they have to, but because they want to—in reproducing the details of a surgical operation, and others who paint ghostly apparitions, the product of their fertile imaginations. Why not? Provided they are made with an honesty of creative purpose and fulfill the instincts of the individual, it is wholly immaterial if many artistic products, both professional and amateur, seem strange and bizarre, for these products may truthfully represent the vision and the dream that lay in the artist's mind. This is neither to defend nor to attack so-called "modern art." Art undertaken in response to an inner urge becomes a creative expression for the individual, irrespective of its excellence when compared with the artificial standards of a profession. The problem, after all, is an individual one in the use of the New Leisure for individually creative purposes.

Like other hobbies and professions, amateur drawing and painting, originally taken up with an open mind, often falls victim to the human tendency toward pedantry. There seems to be something about the artistic expression of an individual's ideas that tends to seek self-glorification, and to attain the stamp of authority by some boasted claim to superiority, although a lack of creative honesty—a desire for sensationalism—is not an exclusive fault of art, either as a profession or a hobby. The amateur who turns to drawing or painting for his leisure and begins to learn something of that vast field upon which he has entered, often tries to excuse his limitations by claiming for them inherent characteristics of superior rightness as opposed to all other channels of thought or interpretation. Particularly in the art of painting, this form of pedantry has taken a strong hold, and often serves as a discouragement to those who, as amateurs, may wish to enter this field. Art, no less than religion, suffers from its Brahmin caste.

179

THE CHALLENGE OF LEISURE

The answer to pedantry in art is the same as that to pedantry elsewhere. True humor and tolerance are human characteristics notable for their rarity, but all the more essential to be cultivated. And, because the use of the New Leisure is an individual matter; because leisure activities are valuable by the very measure of the opportunity they offer to express thoughts and emotions ordinarily suppressed, it is far better that individuality and attempted short-cuts to superiority find expression in leisure activities non-harmful to others than that they should disturb the well-oiled balance of a necessarily regulated economic system. Probably no human being exists who does not possess certain peculiarities, and there is no possibility of controlling the human desire to elevate one's own peculiarities to the position where one need not be ashamed of them. So we must keep in mind that from the point of view of the New Leisure the interpretation that we should give to every activity must be on the basis of its service and value to the performer—its potentialities for bringing recreational release, for diversion of physical and mental powers into channels harmless and non-destructive to the rights of others.

Music is a similar expression of thought, emotion, and creation. Perhaps even more than most of the other arts, it has always been a reflection of national character, and, when that character is restless, elemental, and pioneering, the music of the people will express the same psychological trends. So we have the Jazz Age, which had its birth and still finds its greatest expression in America. But, before the Jazz Age, when we were still an agrarian people, we, too, had our songs that were not far different from the folk songs of other country-dwelling populations, and the songs of toil and lamentation created by Negro slaves are as poignant an expression of character and of environment as any Gypsy dance or Spanish love song.

What will be the music of the New Leisure? We do not know. We only know that, if leisure changes the character of our nation, it will change the character of our music as well. The Machine Age has had and will continue to exert an important influence on music. To the extent that man is the creator of machines, they will ordinarily follow his development rather than lead it, but machines for reproducing music are capable of carrying the message of musical progress, and serve to educate the many to the standards of the best creators. Thus will the character of our music keep pace more readily with our unconscious national character.

Already music of the higher and more advanced type—a type requiring deeper appreciation—seems to be spreading. Symphony orchestras and grand opera, once supported by the few rich, would have failed almost utterly with the depression had not the truly popular demand of radio and phonograph kept them alive. Our leading symphony orchestras are examples of this, and we find that even grand opera is being broadcast at the expense of hard-headed commercial advertisers who make it their business to know what the public wants. We find American composers writing new songs, not all jazz songs, and we even find that the writers of jazz themselves are no longer turning out the blatant, obvious harmonies of the Post-War period. The vast catalogue of American music, ranging from individual sketches through trios, quartets, ballets, to symphonies and operas, is being added to almost daily—not only by those few Americans who may achieve immortality through their compositions, but by increasing numbers of amateur composers. The existence of composers' clubs in many of our larger cities indicates the growth of amateur musical creation.

In addition to appreciation and creation, there
182

is a third element worthy of equal consideration from the standpoint of the New Leisure—this we may term participation. In the actual playing of musical instruments participation seemed to have received a serious setback a few years ago, because of the radio and phonograph, but today the manufacturers of instruments see glimmerings of improvement. For appreciation of music does not seem enough for many human beings. They are impelled to learn to reproduce it themselves, and now that time is no longer at a high premium, there is every likelihood that participation will increase.

In this participative feature lie opportunities for public coöperation and encouragement through recreational centers that may aid in furnishing instruction and assist in the organization of orchestras and choruses. The need for this is well illustrated in the report of a member of the field staff for the National Recreation Association. He instances how an unemployed Italian, a musician twenty-three years old, formed a symphony orchestra of men and boys with a membership of twenty-five, including Italians, Portuguese, and Jews. He secured help in organizing the orchestra in his neighborhood recreation center, where space was furnished for rehearsals. This orchestra has given several concerts, charging ten and fifteen cents admission to cover the cost of the music. The young organizer took just pride in his leadership, and has been so inspired by the success and joy derived from this venture that he has set about organizing a boys' orchestra.

Singing, the natural human expression of music, and undoubtedly the most primitive, has long been recognized as possessing remarkable psychological value, and, for that reason, has often been made to serve dubious ends. The organizers of war employed group-singing to stimulate patriotism; politicians and revolutionists made use of it to create mass loyalty to some individual or cause, and it has been the chief instrument in inducing types of religious hysteria. But singing has potentialities far greater than all of these, for community singing possesses the power to develop a spirit of common interest and affection for one's fellow-man. So it works directly toward the attainment of a national and even a world-wide ideal, for singing possesses a creative power toward attaining that happiness and contentment which are the social aims of mankind.

The art which reaches the greatest number of persons and which occupies the largest proportion of the free hours of the people is that of the theater. It is, likewise, an art the character of which has changed radically in the past two decades. In that period the motion picture has grown from an infant industry producing flickering films of dubious artistic quality to a major industry with frequent flashes of real artistry. In the same time the spoken theater has waned so far as its contact with the people of the whole country is concerned. No longer do touring companies of competent actors and actresses troup the hinterlands with plays of proved caliber. Except for a few of the larger cities, there is no commercial theater, save the motion pictures. The reason lies in the competition of the talkies and the prohibitive cost of maintaining road companies.

Yet there is inherent in most of our people a love of the spoken theater. They fundamentally prefer three dimensions and flesh and blood performers to two dimensions and celluloid actors. The legitimate theater is an art well worth saving, but, for the majority of our people, it will be lost unless that inherent taste for it is stimulated and kept alive. In leisure lies that opportunity.

Today the number of non-professional acting groups may be counted in the hundreds. While some of them are dedicated to that which is bizarre and symbolic and "arty," the vast majority

185

of the groups are interested in presenting performances of plays of proved worth and appeal to the best of their varying abilities. Many of them attain a high standard of acting and staging, presenting a group of plays each season and enjoying a patronage sufficiently large to permit the continued expansion of their activities.

Here, then, lies a use of leisure of distinctly constructive nature. It provides not only opportunity to act, but gives the mechanically-minded members of the group a chance to experiment and to surmount obstacles. A wide variety of interests —carpentry, scenery painting, direction, property managing, business direction, publicity, electrical effects, as well as acting, are combined in any amateur dramatic group. Thousands of people today are either concerned as participants in or active supporters of amateur dramatic groups. They are keeping the spoken stage alive in the hinterlands. Now and then they furnish a recruit to the ranks of the professional theater, or give a talented playwright his first chance at production. But, above all, they are furnishing a valuable use of leisure for their members, a use which merits even wider adoption and greater encouragement.

Perhaps the most definite record of the effect of the New Leisure in its present early stages is

186

found in the public attitude toward literature. Recently, the Library Journal, a publication dedicated to public library management, brought out the significant fact that between 1929 and 1933 a remarkable trend of public interest toward reading had practically doubled the previous use of public libraries. It is quite natural that the first tendency of an individual with leisure time on his hands is to turn to books, but it would be equally natural to assume that without previous training he would give the greatest attention to fiction. This, however, does not seem to be altogether the case—the Milwaukee Public Library, for example, found that, while fiction reading increased by more than half, the popularity of more serious subjects showed an even greater per cent of increase. During this same period the demand for books on natural science, philosophy, and religion almost doubled, while the call for books on social science more than doubled and taxed the capacity of the library to the full.

People with time on their hands want to be entertained; they want to study natural science; they want to develop a philosophy of life, to find some spiritual and religious significance to living; and, increasingly, they want to learn about economics and social progress. Yet the greatest increase of all is shown in the demand for books on music and art, and the important thing here is that sooner or later this reading interest is bound to be interpreted in deeds and action, in a change that will modify our strictly commercial progress not only toward greater social responsibility, but also toward greater national consciousness of esthetic values. This report would seem to be a most significant document, not yet capable of demonstrable results in human actions, but filled with potentialities for the nation's future.

Reading is itself a New Leisure activity of immense portent. From the point of view of absorption and appreciation, literature is a leisure consumer, but it is also a builder that leads constructively toward each and all of the various other leisure-time occupations. It is an integral part of education, and, as such, will necessarily blossom forth into a future related to the character of one's reading. For reading is a part of living, making for the fuller life, not only because of the act of reading itself, but also because of that which may follow out of it.

Like music, literature presents various aspects. Appreciation is one phase, creation another. And creation through writing has been the expression

188

of a human need ever since the art of writing began. It is a foundation stone of education, and the basis of all human development. Writing is an expression of ideas and tends to formulate, clarify, and give purpose and articulateness to thought. Abstract thought, in which literature has its birth, sooner or later reaches the confines of its own limitations and must find expression. Writing offers the ideal outlet for thought. It becomes an urge that takes hold increasingly upon those who recognize it, and often absorbs a whole purpose of life. It becomes an end in itself—a complete existence calling forth all the best thought and the greatest qualities of the writer.

Writing takes its root in the story-telling urge which appears during the childhood of every normal boy and girl. The first thing a child wants to do is to make up and tell a story of his own, for story-telling is almost the first elementary expression of the creative urge. In many it becomes lost and the creative instinct turns to other interests. In many others it is starved by the abuses of education, forced into early channels of conformity, associated with unpleasant tasks, and the result is that the urge to make stories or to write down one's thoughts is all too often suppressed and destroyed. Facility of expression, development of a

189

vocabulary—these are mistakenly treated as subjects of minor importance in the preparation for earning a livelihood, and, if the writing urge survives, it is oftenest because it is too strong to be overwhelmed by our all too common handling of childhood.

Writing requires leisure—much time for thought, for the development of imagination, correlation of ideas, the practice of setting them down in an orderly, attractive way, so that even he who rides may read. Like art and music, writing suffers from a superficial judgment of effectiveness and from an unjust and unnecessary comparison with the standards of genius. But writing is a developable ability. It often sends forth unexpected blossoms in later life, and so offers a tremendously creative activity for the New Leisure, an opportunity open to many thousands who have never suspected its inherent interest and possibilities.

Writing is a broad field, coloring and influencing every occupation and every knowledge of mankind. It may be related to art or music, to agriculture, philosophy, religion, or a hundred other subjects that are in themselves interests and hobbies. But writing is not merely part of any one

190

or all of them—it stands alone to represent the doings and thoughts of mankind, to record the imagination and mental processes of the writer in relation to any or all of life.

Thus do the artistic, musical, and literary potentialities of all life's values center in the New Leisure, wherein there is so much to do that man need never be without activity, but can find opportunity at every turn to make his life far more than it ever could have become in the days when time itself was precious and the world revolved about the necessitous mechanics of making a living. The man with leisure is a free man having opportunity equal to that of any other, and part of that leisure he will devote to his unceasing search for beauty. For beauty, as typified in art, in music, and in the great books of the world, is man's protest against ugliness, and is his compensation against the inequalities of human living. A flight? Perhaps. In certain of its aspects, all art is a flight, but in a far more important sense it offers to equalize our human lot by giving us command over any one of these creative arts. None of us may be as big a man as Shakespeare, but we can stand on his shoulders, and the view, once glimpsed, is unforgettable. It is beauty in its myriad forms that makes man as the gods and

raises him above the exigencies of daily tasks. Art
is man's great contribution to human living, and
the beauty that he is creating transcends life itself, for it is a conscious selection of all the best
life has to offer.

IX

THE NEW LEISURE AND HUMAN
RELATIONSHIPS

NEWTON D. BAKER, speaking on the New Leisure, has referred to the Standard of Thinking in
contradistinction to the Standard of Living. It is
a significant phrase, and holds the essence of a
vast conception. For one thing, it raises the perti-
ment question as to whether or not the majority of
the people in the United States really do much
thinking at all—beyond what is required for the
bread and butter necessities of life. After all, there
is a homely truth in the saying that "man is an
animal who constantly tries to become a vegetable." And in the last analysis most of us flee
from the task of original thinking. The Machine
Age, of course, does not encourage originality. It
fits the world into a physical mold, a standard of
button-pushing to achieve results, and this button-
pushing characteristic pervades the mental field
as well. Our age has become an era of slogans,

shibboleths, and empty formulas, where conformity to standards reaches a kind of common denominator that is, perhaps, not quite at the bottom of the mental scale, but certainly not far above it.

Editors of our daily press and of that flood of magazines which colorfully bespatter the newsstands with elemental appeal frankly recognize that the average mentality conforms to that of about a twelve-year-old child. They pride themselves on "giving to the public what the public wants"—a principle which is itself characteristic of the very type we are discussing. Marital triangles, love nests, and bizarre crimes are offered as sops to minds which apparently have nothing else to think about because civilization somehow runs itself and muddles along without them. Democracy is regarded as a rubber stamp, a sort of privilege like that of a common stockholder in a large corporation, who is supposed to content himself with signing proxies to keep the management in power.

Conformity has its roots deep in Machine Age standardization, but its greatest growth was attained during the late prosperity. It was the watch-word of that intense inflationary period that followed shortly after the Great War and extended until almost 1930. Then, when everything began to crack and the millions of uniformly adolescent minds found themselves unable to cope with disaster, the nation sent up a cry for help and sought frantically for a Moses. But where were the thought, the mentality, and the leadership that the people so sorely needed? True, there were a few who could suggest, and lead, too—a few who possessed constructive ideas, but they were so pitifully, so inadequately few.

The need for dictatorship and the willingness to accept it docilely are the strongest possible evidences of mass weakness, of general mental incompetence, and the stultification of really constructive thought and executive ability. These are the outgrowth of artificially drugged minds, rendered incapable of social vision because they are never called upon to develop anything more than compliance, and are never trained to any destiny higher than that of insentient cogs in a machine. Without a commensurate standard of thinking, the standard of living is but an empty shell supported by a dangerous, vicious circle of routine operations and bound to collapse at a breath. Human standards, in their truest sense, are not to be measured by the yardstick of so many automobiles or radios per capita, or even by the average wages of our workers. Human standards have to do with

195

spiritual things, and must be measured in those terms or not at all.

The poverty of our national standard of thinking is well illustrated in the almost complete loss of the art of conversation. Good conversation is truly an art, requiring its devotees to practise a long list of social virtues—patience, understanding, sympathy, tolerance, intelligence—and demanding, as do all other refinements of civilization, constant exercise to prevent its loss. Good conversation is hard to find nowadays—only a little less hard than during the great prosperity period preceding the depression—for conversation seems to have fallen into the category of hand labor and has been displaced by the machines that do our talking for us. It has become irrelevant, spread thinly and superficially over a variety of topics, and is not necessarily listened to any more than the radio, which is its mechanical substitute.

The radio and phonograph have done more to ruin conversation and original thought than any other development of the Machine Age. Because the radio will drone on, hour after hour, the average American family leaves it running, while some listen half-heartedly and others not at all. If there are important remarks to be made, they have to

196

be shouted in tone and key to drown the mechanical reproduction. And the average person, rather than compete with the stentorian blaring of a loud speaker, lapses into stony silence—another instance of man vanquished by his machine.

Almost any topic on earth may be discussed over the radio, with certain naïve moral restrictions, so that such thoughts as we have may be handed to us cooked and canned, and almost predigested. There is neither incentive to agree or to disagree, to argue, to question, or to convince—the machine does not listen. So, while we have lost the art of talking, we have also lost the art of listening. Gradually we come to pay little more attention to the spoken remarks of our neighbor than we do to the incessant chatter of the machine.

Now, it is not to be assumed that a proper solution lies in abolishing the radio any more than the solution of our economic troubles necessitates a revolutionary abandonment of all the benefits of the Machine Age, with a consequent return to hand labor. Our trouble is simply that we have allowed standards of thinking to become so muddled as to prevent the potential advantages of the Machine Age from reaching their highest value. Our educational standard—our standard of thinking—should, by all means, be much higher today than it was before we had the benefit of mechanical exchange of thought so ready at hand. Instead, our ideals have been lost in an attitude of "laissez-faire" conforming with that low common denominator of mentality already referred to.

Thoughtful conversation between individuals is perhaps the greatest educational medium in the world. Listening is, of course, the theoretical root of learning, but the formation of orderly ideas requires expression; the development of thought requires an interplay, a psychological process wherein the combined value of two or more minds is added. Contentment and happiness are, in part, products of such social exchange, a result of using our inherited and instinctive powers—a phase of creation. From this point of view, thoughtful conversation differs but little from the host of clearly definable and physically created pursuits, and becomes a leisure activity on a par with them.

But conversation possesses the advantage of requiring no paraphernalia, no financial expenditures, and no paternalistic regulation. Good conversation has a distinct therapeutic value as well. In supplying the creative urge with an expression or outlet, it tends to release burdens of worry and care, and so its effects upon health are similar to

198

those of any hobby that we have discussed. It may, as a matter of fact, be a substitute for a hobby or an addition to one. Thoughtful conversation fulfills a psychological need and provides the stimulus of competition. It recognizes mental superiority and acclaims it by way of succinct reward. Thought expressed in conversation is not far removed from similar thought expressed in literature—the one impinges upon the field of the other until the two are complementary, and each appears as a definite classification of a worthwhile New Leisure activity.

But, in addition to all these benefits of conversation, there exists another of greatest social significance. Ralph Waldo Emerson has called conversation "the practice and consummation of friendship." Since human relations have so much to do with our ideal of happiness and contentment, we should not pass by the opportunities afforded by the New Leisure without considering the healthful and psychological values of friendship itself. Friendship may be based upon a mutual sharing of experience, but experience, in the physical sense of doing, is far less an element in this situation than is the sharing of thought. The decadence of conversation has done much to destroy the creational and recreational values of

199

friendship as functions of leisure. For, when mutual exchange and interchange of thought fail, human relations descend to a basis of sharing physical performance and superficial conformity, wherein the values are comparatively shallow, the constructive purpose weak, and the significance toward individual living minimized. So it may become an important function of the New Leisure to develop friendship and make of it a greater force to balance with genuine pleasure the disappointments of living.

What may be said of friendship applies equally to the ties of the home. The sermons and speeches delivered on the subject of family life as the root strength of the nation have been legion. Most of us nominally accept the principle as conforming with ideas we are supposed to possess, but we give it little actual thought. The physical relationships of the family tie are but a small element, readily mechanized, like the age in which we live. They are disregarded and ignored, just as the blare of the radio has taught us to ignore a noise, and yet to feel somehow empty and dissatisfied without it.

An effort to raise our standard of thinking to a plane commensurate with our standard of living is bound to reëmphasize the human relationships of the family and to furnish a definite sustenance

200

upon which this most fundamental and yet delicate of all social human relationships may feed and exist. The home supplies a nucleus from which to build social relationships upon a firm foundation; it offers a place for the creative and recreational opportunities and values of conversation. If there is any meaning at all to the principles and ideals of home life that we all profess to accept, then the home can and will become the irradiating center for the New Leisure and for a fuller living.

The home was once the great educational center. The children who went out from it bore the impress of its character, and their conception of living was that which was given to them by their parents. But the modern home, influenced by intensive urban development and concentration of population exhibited in the apartment house dwelling, possesses shortcomings in other ways than size and physical limitations. Parents, caught up in the rush and restlessness of life at the peak of national prosperity, seemed to be able to find no time to give their children. If Father was away all day, so, also, was Mother, for her engagements had become equally intensive. Yet, what can possibly be a more logical, a more worthwhile use of the New Leisure by parents than to devote part of it to their children, to help them attain a philosophy of living that will bring to them more abundant happiness than that enjoyed by a previous generation? Perhaps the immediate obstacle to this use of the New Leisure in securing a better parent-child relationship is the fact that the parents themselves lack any philosophy of life to impart. It may well be that by reading and thought they themselves will have to acquire a philosophy before they can impart it. At least, there will be no harm done by regarding the home as the place to practice the new conception of human relationships, for, beyond the shadow of any doubt, the home supplies a tangible background and an advantage that no school or institution can ever give.

Recently this fact was brought out in a dramatic way by studies made on children in Soviet Russia—children who had been brought up in institutions and long separated from their parents. Here, in spite of scientific feeding, systematic care, and recreation, it was found that the children were less healthy and had attained less growth than those of similar ages who were brought up in the home. The difference must lie in some social relationship between parent and child that can not, without disastrous results, be dispensed with.

Many modern families that have been lost in

the hurry and rush of the past generation have probably so forgotten how to create the atmosphere that transmutes a dwelling into a home that it will be difficult for them to reëstablish it; but literature has not forgotten; progressive thought has added much to what was previously known, and all this is recorded in book form.

Besides conversation, the tie that has linked groups together from ancient times has been found in literature, and one leisure-time activity for the home, which has been almost forgotten, is reading, particularly reading aloud. In thousands of homes, as well as college classrooms, there still hangs a picture, one of the most famous ever painted, if one may judge by the number of its reproductions. The title is "A Reading from Homer," and the painting shows what was undoubtedly a family or clan group sitting and lying about the reader with his scroll. It serves to remind us, this picture, that in the days of the ancient Greeks such readings and recitals were the primary social use of leisure. Today reading aloud is a form of entertainment seldom employed. Undoubtedly, competition with the radio and other artificial forms of amusement originally displaced reading, largely because these newer ideas were taken up for their novelty and pursued until the old, more substantial habits were forgotten. If you ask the average person to read aloud, you will usually get the answer that he has no time, or that he does not read well—both invalid excuses. Ability in all things grows from practice, and the ability to read aloud is an art that can be developed to the pleasure of reader and listener alike. It possesses many of the advantages of conversation in that it unites minds in a single thought, and, if the thought itself is worthwhile, it is the more effectively received because of the number of minds listening together. We do not have to turn to the past for all our ideals, but, where we can find something worth doing, such as reading aloud, something which applies the New Leisure to constructive improvement of both the individual and the family tie, the revival of an old custom needs no greater justification.

The artificial prosperity which characterized the period just before the depression of 1930 and the years that followed had a tremendously destructive influence upon the home. The scramble after wealth, the orgy of spending, drew every member of the family into a maelstrom of vicarious occupations and amusements, while, at the same time, the psychological revolt against the restrictions of prohibition seemed to engulf all ages in a secretive and furtive individualism that was opposed to society as a whole, and particularly to those manifestations that had their foundation in home and family relationships. Home labor-saving devices and purchased luxuries at the same time lightened the load of domestic work and responsibility. Families that had never been able to employ servants suddenly believed themselves able to afford them, while others increased their domestic staffs. As a partial result of all this, the sharing of work, always one of the strongest home ties and one of the greatest influences for the development of character, lost its hold.

It was unfortunate for everyone concerned, but more particularly for the children. No outside educational process was available or could be developed as a substitute for the responsibility and character-building values of visible and practical daily tasks at home. Expensive entertainments, offering popular allurement, might substitute for simple home games and pleasures, but they really offered no improvement as a source of true happiness and contentment. Indeed, one is led to believe that even had the inflationary period of prosperity continued, some reaction would surely have developed, for it was a period that contained within itself the seeds of its own destruction. Indeed, a reaction was already beginning to show evidence among the more intelligent people when the great bubble burst.

What the bursting of that bubble has done to home and family relationships is already evident in the survey of the leisure activities of five thousand urban people, that we have already spoken of. For those whose security was taken away, all elements of true leisure vanished. Worried and desperate, these people could not play at all. Again and again replies to the questionnaires bore some brief statement that it was impossible even to think of anything beyond the imminence of starvation or loss of home; families were separated with no ties to bind them until the destruction was complete. But for those families whose fundamental security was not destroyed, and for whom remained a reasonable degree of employment, the story is different. A section of the questionnaire was devoted to changes in leisure activities—to things done more or less than they had previously been done—and here it immediately appeared that those changes showed a re-centering about the home. There was more leisure time devoted to conversation, letter writing, caring for home grounds and gardens, cooking, dressmaking, and card games. There were more home dancing parties, more playing of musical instruments, caring for pets and pitching horseshoes in the back yard. An increase in newspaper reading and in more serious reading was everywhere noticeable.

Obviously, these new activities—particularly dressmaking, cooking, and gardening—were first of all the result of grim necessity. Lacking money to pay a gardener or cook, householders found themselves obliged to do the work themselves, and women who could no longer afford to buy ready-made clothes were forced by circumstances to learn to sew. But, though at the outset these activities were nothing more than inescapable tasks, each one of them entails creative effort, and somewhere between their adoption and the reporting of them as real leisure-time activities, the satisfaction that comes from accomplishment had transformed them from mere labor to leisure-time recreation. And it was this very turning back into the home for recreation on the part of those who still possessed some degree of security that constituted the budding of the New Leisure.

The legend of the home as the bulwark of the state originated among an agrarian people. Family ties were closely knit, not only by bonds of affection and common memories and tradition, but, most of all, by community of interest—the sharing of the work of home maintenance, the division of the tasks of livelihood. Thus, so far as the New Leisure may decree and permit a return to the soil on the subsistence homestead basis, the human relationships of the home are bound to be thrust upon the consciousness of the new homesteaders. What they can make of it, what it can produce, in terms of that happiness and contentment which all the world is seeking, will depend, however, upon something more than mere physical sharing, for, as we have pointed out, subsistence homesteading in the New Leisure does not preclude a supplementary introduction of other leisure purposes and occupations into the home. Music, art, and scientific hobbies have already been touched on, but more essential than any of these is the interchange of thought and ideas. Through this interchange will arise a clearer conception of the home as a unit in the whole social structure, and by means of it will arise a constructive interest in the social body. For, just as the human cell is a biological unit in that great integration making up the physical body, so is the family a social-economic unit without which no form of society can be successfully integrated or very long endure.

208

HUMAN RELATIONSHIPS

We may not close a consideration of leisure occupation, particularly in connection with human relationships, without referring to the existence of those spiritual values which transcend the definable characteristics of human activity. By what name we may call these spiritual values is of no particular importance to their practical application. But there does remain the inescapable fact that conscious or sub-conscious idealism adds a constructive element to any pursuit and yields a definitely beneficial value to the pursuer. It is on the plane of this conception that philosophical, psychological, and religious thought meet, all pointing to the fact that service to a fellow-man or fellow-men reacts directly upon the performer. It is the bread cast upon the waters; it is the higher, spiritual economics of the Golden Rule. In some manner that we do not clearly understand, spiritual qualities seem to influence even physical health, and they create the last and highest link of a balanced life—the link that is most important of all.

Much of the revolt expressed against our civilization today is the result of the fact that civilization has endeavored to reduce spiritual values to formulas as mechanical and as conformative as any of the other acts of living; but such mechanical conformity is not within the purview of our discussion. Except for specific individuals who may choose a nominally spiritual activity as their profession or their leisure occupation, the name of the endeavor really matters nothing. Sermons from the pulpit or rostrum are a generally acknowledged form, undeniable as to spiritual value for at least the preacher who delivers them with honest intent. A similar honesty of purpose may also prove the measure of value to those who listen; but a belief that performance, or conformance, more or less popularly defined as religion, constitutes a monopoly of all spiritual values is merely a treading of the well-worn conformity road. It is an expression of inherited compliance, rather than an attempt to set up a standard of thinking which can transcend the limitations of a muddling past. Public service, in positions of high authority or low, may attain the highest spiritual values of human relationship, but only if those values are honestly sought. The curious fact in the spiritual essence of human relationship seems to be that each smallest human service or interest in helping a fellow-man offers a thrill of creation, non-physical, and non-definable, but epitomizing whatever it is that makes the individual human life happy, contented, and complete.

HUMAN RELATIONSHIPS

Nature interests, outdoor sports, hobbies—all possess potentialities of human relationship in addition to their directly creative functions. It is the development of these potentialities that relates all New Leisure activities, one to the other, and supplies the most usable value of their service to mankind. Human society, being but the sum-total of individuals, is the gainer by the progress of each component toward a common goal. This was the end for which the founders of the American Constitution set their aim. This is the true goal of society throughout the world, and it is clearly the great opportunity which is now offered to us through the New Leisure. To quote from the National Commission on the Enrichment of Adult Life, "What the American people do in their spare time henceforth will largely determine the character of our civilization."

X

THE NEW LEISURE AND EDUCATION

WE AMERICANS are the most restless people in the world. Bearing the blood of pioneers, the inherited seeds of dissatisfaction and change garnered from every quarter of the globe, we are descended from those who have hurled themselves into the face of a wilderness and transformed it into something we now call civilization. At this civilizing process we have long labored, building up complexities and complications that we hope and suppose to be order. With hands and brains we have created, but, somehow, as we turn and look back upon our progress, the result offers us neither satisfaction nor peace.

The curse of restlessness is still upon us—there seems no refuge from it. In the past outlets always existed for those upon whom this curse was strongest. They could seek new territories; they could invade frontiers and fight Indians; they could make war. To be sure, this last gateway still stands open, and beckons many to international quarrels or internal revolutions—those brief but often sanguinary conflicts that offer to the maladjusted respite from failure or release from social and economic impasses. And yet war itself has lost much of its allure as a vent for anti-social instincts, for we have "civilized" war to the point where it is no longer fun. Modern war making will not allow us to fight as individuals, but enslaves us to machines of destruction.

Now, it would be a facile observation to say that we shall never have permanent peace or contentment until we conquer this restlessness; that we can never attain to any really stable economic system until we have learned the arts of leisure and thus idyllically mended our ways—until we have become different, and in the Biblical sense, "by taking thought, add a cubit to our stature." But, alas, so sudden a change is for the present, at least, a futile dream. The human organism is not tolerant of such abrupt transition. Take the drug away from an addict too abruptly, and he becomes a raving maniac. Deprive a working man of even part of his work, and you intensify his restlessness. Eventually you may turn him into a tramp or some even more dangerous predator on society. No, the only compensation for activity is still

213

more activity, and it is this situation that we must face in the New Leisure. Our problem, then, is to supply in adequate measure legitimate activities for the energies of a congenitally restless people, while, at the same time, for purely economic reasons, cutting down each individual's working hours, so that the world's available work may be spread among a great number of persons.

A study of the problem of leisure activity points clearly to the impossibility of properly directing leisure in any sense without the complement of widespread education. Education, indeed, must form not merely an aid to recreational direction, but must serve as its very foundation and bulwark. A comparatively few people who have had the benefits of broad cultural training and experience will, of course, not require outside direction to take up hobbies and interests and to pursue them with happiness and contentment. But minds that have been trained primarily to make a living will, as a general thing, prove incapable of expanding to the wise management of free time on their own initiative. For people who fall into this category—particularly for those trained to make a livelihood in commerce or in industry—agricultural and outdoor pursuits might provide ideal leisure-time activities. Thus, they would balance

214

factory and city environment by intimate contact with the soil, and offer opportunity for individual initiative as a wholesome change from the stultifying task of machine-tending. But these leisure-time activities, we have already seen, are in the majority of cases unavailable to the very groups who need them most urgently—the millions who are handicapped by living in an environment where agricultural and outdoor pursuits are quite impossible. Where farming, gardening, or nature interests fail to supply a full complement of activity for a happy and contented existence, it will be necessary not only to show people what to do, but, also, to begin at the beginning and explain to them every phase of how to do it. And even then it is unlikely that the average laborer or clerk will know what he wants to do in the first place.

Education such as that provided by the majority of our public schools and extended into many of our universities, fails to open the doors of the mind on anything approximating a broad scale. Rather it has tended to restrict and disregard everything that does not lead toward some definite end, an end usually connected with earning a livelihood or with the maintenance of purely artificial social standards. Education has been too much preoccupied with the problem of how to

215

make a living, and not enough with the far more important problem of how life should be lived.

Yet in every week there are more than a hundred waking hours to be accounted for, only a part of which are occupied with the mechanics of livelihood. Indeed, if the time dedicated to working should be restricted to a forty-hour week, we can readily see that sixty hours, or nearly two-thirds of the time not needed for sleep, will be free time, available to us to make the most of, and even deducting a generous number of hours for eating and other physical needs, the hours of labor would be practically equaled by the hours available for leisure. Why, then, should education limit itself to the uses of half a life only?

There is no doubt that educators the nation over are giving serious thought to this very problem. Recently the National Recreation Association conducted a survey and published the findings in a book entitled, "The New Leisure Challenges the Schools." In it a comprehensive attempt has been made to study our educational problem, with particular reference to the public schools. The interest of educators in training for the use of leisure dates back many years, and in 1918 the National Education Association accepted training for the worthy use of leisure as one of the seven objectives of secondary education, while the National Congress of Parents and Teachers followed with a similar resolution only a little later. Groups of schools and individual schools have taken this principle as their model and have produced many outstanding examples of leisure education.

The great weakness of our public education lies in the fact that there is no single unified plan, no simple way of attacking the problem as a whole, and the reason for this is because we have no such thing as a single school system in this country. The nation is not a unit; neither are the individual states, and schools are organized, financed, and governed almost exclusively on a local basis. Educational units derive their financial support from an antiquated system, whereby the expense of education is paid by the land of the local region. Wherever that land is valuable, where people are prosperous and able to pay taxes, education prospers and is able to include many "extras" of more or less dubious utility, together with many truly progressive movements. And it is there we find leisure-time education at its best.

On the other hand, where many people are concentrated in a single neighborhood that lacks valuable taxable land, the schools are poor financially. So this haphazard, hit-or-miss system results in the converse of all that is most necessary for a broad, integrated attack upon the leisure-time educational problem. Congested regions, where clerks and laborers live, where education for leisure time is most needed, are most lacking in ability to furnish the child with that cultural background which will enable him to adapt himself to a standard of happy and contented living.

The organization of education, and more particularly its financial support, are the weakest links in our whole problem. We find recent attempts to organize school systems within the state and place them upon a better financial basis, independent of local regional taxation, and it is absolutely essential that every state must sooner or later follow this plan. Criticism of failure to provide better education fails to be constructive unless it can also point out some means to obtain it. Our school systems have been regarded as extravagant, and in many instances there is no doubt that extravagance has existed, particularly in building costs, but the New Leisure is bound to force upon the nation a growing realization that education, the bulwark of the American system, must become more of a bulwark than ever, and inescapably will require even larger expenditures than in the past. There will have to be more

218

teachers—more and better teachers for each pupil enrolled. These teachers of the future must be given more thorough training in a wide variety of fields, and most of them will need a broader cultural background and a much more comprehensive outlook upon life. Thus, the need for a better educational system extends back of the primary and secondary schools to normal schools, teachers' colleges, and, ultimately, to the great universities.

Naturally, the cost of education is bound to be greatly increased by such additions in quantity and quality of teachers. Good education is already expensive. At present the financially harassed school boards can not consider recommendations of even the best authorities. The most we can hope to accomplish immediately is to stimulate a demand for better education to the point where eventually it can be translated into legislation and into a willingness to accomplish at least a limited form of financial paternalism. The best that any organizations or interested individuals with a concept of public obligation can do is to call repeated attention to the essential importance of the problem, and to show that this whole question of the New Leisure, with its social-economic aspects, must be faced. We shall have to demonstrate that the wise use of the New Leisure is so inextricably

219

entwined with every other great social and economic problem that progress can be made only on all alike and equally, for it is impossible to regard the New Leisure problem and its concomitant educational problem as mere furbelows of a "New Deal." A reorganization of education is as much an essential part of the "New Deal" as are the regulation of industry and the stimulation of commerce. Unless the people of the nation are given a new purpose in life and a new ideal to follow, all the commercial and other economic plans of the brainiest "brain-trusts" in the world are doomed to failure.

Public education, according to the American principle, was from its inception the most paternalistic concept in the American Constitution. It began with the recognition that education was the duty of the state to promote and support, but this has fallen short of its fulfillment because of compromise with anti-paternalistic public sentiment. Nevertheless it has been the accepted province of paternalism since the creation of the United States of America.

In our zeal to avoid the pitfalls of too much centralized authority and in our fear of government interference with family life, education became a local community project only, and in so doing lost the power to progress beyond local demand and local ability to meet the cost. Since the election of Franklin Roosevelt as President, paternalism on the part of the Federal Government has been offered as the solution for all the nation's ills. It has been tried in connection with a myriad of social questions, and has been blamed for a thousand newly appearing social troubles. Whether or not paternalism is being overdone, history alone can say, but one thing is sure—so far as education is concerned, there is no other way out. It alone can now be called on to enable education to meet its new problems.

Yet it must be recognized that just as all public service is not necessarily political, so all support and assistance to education need not be exclusively governmental. The National Education Association, which has done so much in pointing the way toward expanding education to meet present-day problems, is, fortunately, neither government-controlled nor government-financed. The National Recreation Association and the American Nature Association, which are devoting their efforts to a solution of leisure-time problems, are both privately supported and endowed. A host of other organizations and voluntary committees are in a similar situation.

It would be extremely unfortunate if paternalism were ever carried to the extent of stereotyping educational methods. It was this very fear that resulted in the creation of our separate school systems at the very beginning, and, although the danger of rubber-stamp education is as great today, if not greater than ever before, government support of education need not imply government control. Essentially, the two are as different as white from black, and, when we speak of paternalism in regard to education and the need for increased attention to this problem, we are thinking primarily of the *financing* of education rather than its planning and management by the government or by the body politic. The world today is full of examples of controlled educational policies—examples which are in every way un-American. Nevertheless, without a new method of financing education as a whole, it is not to be expected that education for the use of leisure time can make any substantial progress.

Many public schools that can afford to do so have already begun to meet the leisure problem. They have encouraged manual training, handicrafts, and science of a sort, all leading directly toward the development of creative mechanical hobbies. They have encouraged music and art, looking toward the foundations of a truer appreciation, and, at the same time, developing talents of individual expression. Organized sports have been initiated under professional direction instead of being left to the chance individual initiative of recess or after-school hours. Reading, literature, and dramatics are presented as cultural and creative opportunities for fuller living. The mere additions of new subjects to the curriculum is important, since it gives to geography and history a vital interest, a place in the vivid pageantry of life, a flavor that connects them with social progress as a foundation for the understanding of economics.

There is no more fundamental approach to the future wise use of leisure than through the proper teaching of what is commonly called Nature Study. Here is embodied a myriad of potential interests for the future. The study of plant life leads to gardening, agriculture, forestry, botany, and micro-biology, chemistry and physics; animal life study leads to every interest that has its source here, to outdoor recreation, hunting and fishing, to advanced zoölogical pursuits that are essential to conservation. Bird and insect study, related to the world about us, carry a host of potential implications for later use. In Nature Study we meet first

223

with geology, with the origin of the world and of man himself, and we are led on to anthropology, paleontology, and all those related fields where science is still pioneering, and where unknown universes may still exist for future generations to discover and to add to the sum total of human knowledge—universes without number, for astronomy, first met through the study of the stars, includes the incredible immensity of all that lies beyond our tiny planet. In knowing the winds and weather, we touch upon another frontier where aviation needs the pioneering of future generations, where the effects of wind and rain and their causes govern the very life of mankind. Yes, the realm of nature is far wider than the bird and the brook, and the knowledge to be extracted forms the basis of professions and businesses that the casual observer little suspects. Secrets of nature, previously hidden but now brought to light, have changed what formerly appeared fundamental axioms, and secrets as yet unrevealed will just as surely change our present world in a number of unsuspected ways.

A survey of Nature Education in the public schools throughout the United States was made in 1931 by the American Nature Association and published in *Nature Almanac*. It shows much progress and many shortcomings.

In 1934 the National Recreation Association, extending the field of education for the New Leisure, published the report entitled "The New Leisure Challenges the Schools," already referred to. In it are given both good and bad examples of the curricula of public schools, not only in Nature Study, but also in Physical Education, Literature, Dramatics, Music, Art, Handicrafts, Social Training, and various extra-curricular activities.

In shaping education for service to the New Leisure, it must be kept in mind that the ability to select and to choose activities with the greatest potentialities for continued interest is of the utmost importance. Adults, no less than children, are prone to respond to temporary influences from the outside, as well as to instinctive tastes from within. Vacillating preference, a dilettante attitude, is actually negation of true choice, and concentration and determination are qualities that must be cultivated early in life, or they are lost forever. So it is not merely the subject matter of teaching that counts, but the methods used and the character of the teacher. The content matter must be made as interesting and vital as possible —it must be related to life within the vision of

225

the pupil, and must call forth an expression of latent instincts instead of affording merely a rote of memorized process. Faddism is a danger to be avoided, for it carries with it an appeal to do that which others are doing—and for no other reason. It is an external stimulus usually unrelated to individual qualifications, and so begets the early lagging that overtakes all interests without deep roots.

There are a few well known and fundamental principles for governing a complete life. Mental and physical interests and activities must develop and maintain some kind of reasonable balance. The brain worker should learn to do something with his hands. The physical laborer needs occupation for thought to direct it in complementary channels. In school it is possible to teach the child to distinguish between the imaginative world and the real one. Recreation through the eye, the kind of passive witnessing that creates dreams of substitution, is not to be condemned as valueless, but must be considered in relation to the life of each individual. It forms a balance to original thought and to physical work, but for the average healthy man or woman it can not be an entire substitute for either. Under wise tutelage the child can be taught to see this difference, and can then, in after life, reap imaginative stimulus from the deeds of others, while translating it into active and effective usefulness for himself.

The protagonists of so-called Progressive Education have been urging this for some years. Their theories are constantly finding a new and firmer foundation, a basis that will appeal more strongly to the everyday citizen. The sudden coming of the New Leisure clarified the goal which the Progressives have already set—the conception of education as a means of developing life interests in addition to and separate from the earning of a livelihood. But this is far more than a victory for a group of theorists. It is a combination of economically caused circumstances which actually removes this so-called Progressive Education entirely out of the realm of theory and makes it a practical problem of human existence.

For we find now that our old, orthodox educational methods, producing lopsided individuals trained in a single talent or specialized skill to the exclusion of all other development, are no longer able to cope with a changed social and economic environment. If we wish to keep from falling hopelessly behind in what Wells calls "the race between education and catastrophe" we must plan from now on to educate the whole man, to educate him for leisure as well as for livelihood, by teaching him to exercise his own resourcefulness and adaptability, to develop such specialized skills as he may need on his own initiative and through his own efforts, and to attain a mutual adjustment with his mental and physical environment.

And so, while Progressive Education has already permeated extensively into elementary education and is now struggling vigorously for a footing in secondary schools, it will receive new impetus to carry it over its present obstacle and up into the colleges and universities. At present there is a pretty definite line of cleavage between curricular and extra-curricular activities on the college campus, yet repeatedly we hear of thoughtful students who attribute even greater value to these extra-curricular experiences than to the subjects actually credited toward a degree. Is it not probable, then, that the New Leisure may require an entire reclassification of educational values all along the scale? May not the New Leisure make necessary in the pedagogic field what Nietzsche demanded fifty years ago for humanity as a whole —a transvaluation of all values? For if earlier cultural training introduces the child to a wide field of constructive human occupations and pur-

228

suits from the point of view of living rather than of livelihood, it would seem that the college must continue the development and offer an equally broad program. College years are assumed to offer the first practical divergence of choice along present cultural lines, but should not the college curriculum give recognition to wider fields of advanced study and specialization in preparation for life itself?

The principle of Adult Education is also an important part of the Progressive creed. School and college years, as they are now understood, are so lamentably short that education, if it is to include a greatly expanded program, will of necessity have to extend into the adult years. And, after all, the New Leisure gives both time and purpose to this very principle. Leisure hours can be devoted to study for the definite purpose of learning leisure use. The goal is certainly quite as definite and the value quite as understandable as in teaching the three R's to young children. But how will this adult education be supported, in order to be available for all? Is there any reason for the arbitrary limitation of publicly financed educational centers, so that youth alone shall be served? As a matter of fact, already a few educational institutions have provided courses for adults, and more

229

will surely follow. Many proposals for adult education have been tendered, covering ages from sixteen to sixty. Based on the CCC camps, and on the assumption that the next few decades will see a great increase in subsistence homesteading, plans have been advanced to train city as well as country boys in rural camps where eight hours a day will be devoted to practical work projects and to the best individual use of leisure. Still another type of rural school proposed is modeled after the English village-school, where instruction is not only provided for children, but where their elders may also find all the facilities now centered in community houses, and may undergo training for the variety of skills needed on farms, from carpentry and shingling to shepherding, and even plumbing.

In his much read book, Professor Pitkin has maintained that most of us are not ready really to live until we reach the age of forty. That may be more literally true than we have imagined. Certainly, leisure-time educational courses for adults might well extend over a period of years, continually enriching the possibilities of life, until in a very true sense the better part would reach us after the age of forty had been passed.

PART THREE

A FEW WORDS IN CONCLUSION

XI

LEISURE—AN ECONOMIC SOLUTION

ALL through these pages we may at times have wandered and digressed, but always we have returned to the central thought of leisure. Let the fever chart of capitalism, socialism, fascism, communism, go up and down as it will. These are no more than the transitory symptoms of our striving, unstable scheme of things. They come and go, but among all this moving flux of ephemeral "isms" one great, undeniable fact remains—mankind as a whole can produce more than mankind consumes.

It is with this basic, fundamental truth that the book before you has to do, and it is this fundamental truth that is the father of leisure and of the problem that leisure has brought. For, as this surplus of human production increases through the discoveries of science, many new products come and go, but one product alone continues to appear in ever-increasing quantities and is destined to alter the course of humankind. That product is leisure. It depends upon no political system and no religious teaching or moral belief. Here in the United States it is not dependent upon the continuance of any New Deal. Regardless of all these things it remains a fact, immense and incontrovertible, demanding to be recognized and to be dealt with.

This social-economic fact, leisure, is bound to have an inescapable effect upon future social trends—an effect which no man can map out in advance. For social progress is like a raindrop on the windowpane of a rapidly moving train. It follows no definitely predictable course. Its route is influenced by gravity, by wind pressure, by the direction of the track itself, and by endless vibrations. Like the raindrop, social progress pursues a composite course which is the physical result of a thousand purposeful shoves and a billion accidental jugglings. Meanwhile, the latest generation of New Dealers, with their ideas of a planned economy, seek to plot and direct the course of this drop, hoping to pilot the ship of state so definitely that of necessity it will follow the route of a mathematical formula. But what is the route? If they are socialists, it must be socialism that they want and plan to secure. If they are communists,

234

with ideals following the type of planned economy Russia has already put into effect, then communism may be their goal.

But, whether they be socialists or communists, fascists or filial descendants of the Wild Jackass, they show transcendent wisdom in not mentioning their goal by name, for names and slogans loom out of all proportion to the American mind, and what a thing is called will often engender a battle far more bitter than the essence of the thing itself. In the Southern States, one has but to call a man a Yankee to defeat his chances of political office. Yet what constitutes a Yankee? Seventy years ago, when carpet-baggers overran the South, the name may have stood for a real and very practical symbol of all the hatred and bitterness the invaders aroused. Today one would be hard put to define what it really means. Yet the word has become a badge of opprobrium, a symbol outlasting the thing it stood for.

If such a quarrel over a name can last for seventy years and more, how much more bitterly can we become confused over the titles of all the various schemes put forward as theoretical cures for the economic and social distress of the present day? It was Shakespeare who first said that a rose by any other name would smell as sweet, but practical American politics has refuted the famous proverb. To the average mind the fragrance and the appellation are inseparable, and, if a thing isn't called a rose, well, it isn't a rose, and that's all there is to it.

So perhaps one of the first uses we Americans could put our leisure to is to teach ourselves to rise above mere slogans. Leisure time should give us an opportunity to reflect upon the vital differences between nominal and actual as a part of our new standard of thinking. And perhaps, if enough thinkers can be found, we may in time achieve a new standard that will help us to know what we want and to seek it free from prejudice, to look beneath the mere name for whatever there is of truth and desirability in both practice and action. For it is an unpleasant but undeniable fact that the great majority of actions are carried out with our prejudices, not with our judgment. We declare war, elect our rulers and political parties with our emotions, and, until we learn really to think, and not merely to "emote," the soap-box orator and the Fourth of July political stentor will continue to sway us and blind us to the real essentials of rational living.

Like a thousand other sound and useful ideas, real understanding will be left to history, wherein the perspective of the years will enable future generations to look back and smile upon the superficial character of our most bitter wrangles, in much the same way that many can now look back at John Brown's Raid, at the Whiskey Rebellion, and all those other strange but typical American outbursts that seemed so vital and overshadowing at the time, yet were only vital through having been the last straw that engendered bloodshed and revolt.

Who could tell in 1933 how long President Roosevelt's "New Deal" would last? Some of its most honest supporters frankly admitted the probability of a return or a reaction, probably under the slogan of "Back to Normalcy." Who could really support the underlying principles of planned economy and not admit the sure occurrence of vital mistakes which would at least temporarily ruin the whole conception? He who might have foretold the developments of the past, or he who today would dare to predict the future would have to be omniscient, and, unfortunately, the only recognized Omniscient Being ceased from delivering his lithographic mandates when Moses in a moment of petulance smashed the Ten Commandments.

The salient facts which one who is far from

237

omniscient may endeavor to interpret can not be set down in any terminology lest that terminology convey the prejudice of an arbitrarily named class, and so be misinterpreted. All that may be said is that which seems to be undeniable—namely, that the struggle for individual security continues and advances, winning minor victories, receiving minor setbacks, but always going forward. That same struggle is still confronted with the fundamental inequalities of man—the restless craving for self-expression, the demand for individualism, the need for opportunity. Even those who crusade most vigorously for social regimentation achieve their individuality in the crusade, and find their opportunity in demanding regimentation. The leader of any regimented system—call it fascism, socialism, or the like—is a leader because he is an individualist. He is winning for himself—or believes that he is winning—honor, power, personal success. In the final analysis, individualism in the social-economic field triumphs by suppressing the individualism of others. It feeds on a cannibalistic diet, and denies its own principles in the very act of achieving them.

When we reason thus, we find ourselves cynics, pessimists, or misanthropes who arrive at last, like the unstoppable object, at the impassable barrier.

238

Apparently, we have exhausted the potentialities of social-economic reasoning and got nowhere. We are unable to do anything, because there is nothing worth doing.

Now, there is a certain amount of this sentiment prevalent in every political opposition—opposition that decides to try to solve the problems of progress by ignoring them or by patriotic platitudes that preach of "good old capitalism," while the American eagle screams on the sidelines. It is the sort of thing that leads to the kind of reasoning that demands one of our periodic "Return-to-Normalcy" debauches.

Nevertheless there is an undeniable virtue in looking backwards, if only for the happiness to be gained from observing the comparatively straight furrow in the plowed field behind us. Reactionists and conservatives alike are individualists, and only as long as we recognize the fact that individualism is an innate and ineradicable human quality can we make any forward progress in a social-economic direction. After all, it is a good thing that we have the American pioneer to point to. He is in our blood oftener than we recognize. We must admit his presence and reckon with him in all our plans, for we can not kill him—that would be self-destruction.

239

THE CHALLENGE OF LEISURE

It is leisure that saves us from the impossible choice between two equally unacceptable alternatives—complete regimentation and suicidal individualism. If leisure is the product, the sure result of civilization, it is also the saving grace, the element that alone may protect mankind from a self-imposed debacle—from being swallowed up by the very machine his brains have created. Leisure is the best guarantee of security because it tends to make some degree of regimentation tolerable, always provided leisure itself is not regimented, but left for the free expression of the individual within us. Leisure is the opportunity for individualism—the opportunity to live, to do and make, according to the dictates of self-expression. In the world of production alone man exists in a vicious, sinister circle, but in the world of leisure he may truly live. It is in leisure that civilization will find its justification. It is the only excuse for civilization, and unless the manifest advantages of leisure outweigh the ills of a machine age, civilization as we now understand it is inevitably doomed. And rightly so, for only in terms of human welfare can the merits of any human system be judged. Leisure, then, is a missing element that may serve to balance the machine and keep it running.

240

But leisure's real *raison d'être* lies not in being a justification of the Machine Age—it has a higher task than that. Through leisure we must achieve a new standard of living and a new concept of a standard of living. Not so much do we need new or revised physical standards, but new psychological standards. That which makes life happy and contented does not consist in a quota of possessions and things, but in an attitude of mind. Fill our lives with enough of doing and making and creating, and the physical standards at once become secondary, and, as such, easily controllable. Mozart, in his attic, knew no difference between poverty and palace, but he lived more truly and fully than millions of others. And, if we can not all be endowed with genius, at least a touch of philosophy will more than a little compensate. The strangest part of all that is that this philosophy is the one solvent of the insuperable. It is the one sure means of reducing the world of production and competition to practical limits in which the physical lack of balance will be compensated for.

But philosophy, like every high art, like every régime of sane living, must be learned. The present generation must also learn a new attitude toward activities that are non-productive in the old

economic sense, and in some cases even leisure
activities themselves must be learned. Only by a
greatly expanded educational program can all this
be accomplished. We must achieve a program that
will not only provide future generations with resources for happiness, but will come to the rescue
of the present mature generation, whose teachers,
complacently oblivious of any approaching leisure
problem, were as a consequence equally oblivious
of any need for wider education. Education is the
very essence of our solution. Education is the *sine
qua non* of any adequate solution of the problem
that has been brought about by an abundant leisure—this strange commodity that has such overwhelming potentialities for either discontent or
happiness, for social or anti-social living.

For leisure, after all, is a commodity—the most
important that all our centuries of civilization
have produced—and like the raindrop on the windowpane, which shifts back and forth as the re-
sultant of many forces, but always tending in the
direction of gravity, so leisure moves in obedience
to very sure and certain trends. It appears suddenly in great abundance, and then is dissipated,
lessened, almost gone, but returns again inevitably, and with each return is stronger and fuller,
and more an integral part of the very pattern and

texture of our national life. For leisure is the surest trend of civilization, and in any realistic summation of the future it must be taken into consideration just as fully as the world reckons with food supplies and monetary standards.

Alas for those economists who see only in terms of money and exchange! The world, although it needs their qualities of mind, can not live upon them alone. They are the social chemists who have resolved the world into two elements—production and consumption. And they would put these elements together again to make life, only to find that their futile synthesis does not work, and the result is chaos. Why? Because the human elements have run out and escaped. Part of the eternal by-product has been forgotten and left upon the shelf in bottles labeled "Individualism", "Pioneer Instinct", and "Essence of Philosophy". But these have all been so incompletely isolated that they creep back into the supposedly perfect mixture and prevent the final success of every experiment.

Leisure is the universal solvent for all these products that conflict with a workable synthesis. Let the social-economic chemists use it, direct it, stimulate and encourage its growth until leisure draws in and makes use of all that troublesome

243

surplus. Then and then alone is it possible to balance the gold and the products which it symbolizes. Leisure is an indispensable part both of economics and of social existence—it is the greatest of all the challenges to the leaders of civilization.